Confident Networker

By

Simone Douglas

Cover design: Nikki Averill
Typesetting: Clockwork Graphic Design
Printing: Printed in Australia

Published by Peritia Press

Contents

Foreword

Networking does not come naturally to most people. It is a learned skill, and it requires confidence in yourself and trust in others. It requires that you are open to helping others and to allowing others to help you. When Simone asked me to write the foreword to her second book, *The Confident Networker*, I did not hesitate to say yes. Even before I read it, I knew that the book would not be based on theory, it would reflect the way that Simone lives her life and runs her businesses.

Simone does not hesitate to ask her network for what she wants or needs, and she allows them to help her. She gives you sound strategies on asking for what you want because she lives it. This is precisely how she got a fantastic pub, The Duke of Brunswick, where she has created the best place to network in all of South Australia, turning a 162-year-old pub into one of the most diverse networking locations in the city, where she caters to a variety of local networks and appetites.

The value that you will find in this book will come from your active engagement with it. Quality networking takes strategy, goals, diversity, practice, target markets, curiosity, and time. So often, people who are out networking are usually doing willy nilly networking all over town, with no idea what they are doing right or wrong. They have no plan, and they do not have the tools to measure their outcomes. They often find out that they are popular around town, but still making very little money. There is value in time, and if you are wasting time running around networking without a plan or system it is a very expensive activity, not only financially, but also in opportunity cost.

What Simone teaches you in this book is what she practices in her life and all of her businesses. She gives you great examples of what she has done, and then gives you actionable steps that you can implement. With this book, your desire, and practicing what you learn, you will become a confident networker who will not only be able to build your business and enrich your life, you will also be able to help others develop their businesses and improve their lives.

Hazel Walker, Author of the New York Times Best Seller *Business Networking and Sex*

Introduction

Becoming A Circle

My business was three months old when a guy I had fired from a hotel six years before invited me to go to his BNI meeting, because he'd seen on Facebook that I'd started a new company.

My first question was, 'Why are you helping me? I fired you!' Admittedly, I had fired him nicely. We came to an agreement that it wasn't the right job for him. Even so, it seemed strange that he was offering to help me.

There is no doubt that he is single-handedly responsible for everything that has happened in my life since that day. By inviting me to a networking event, he was opening up a whole new world of possibilities. This is because the one thing I could do really well was to make friends, and networking is all about making friends. You have to care about people enough to want to help them. When you're networking, if you don't care about people you're not going to get very far.

Keep Your Bridges Intact

The importance of caring about people circles back to the way in which I fired the guy from the hotel. If I hadn't cared about him, I could have just kicked him to the kerb. However, because I recognised that he wasn't a bad person, he was just a bad fit for the job, it meant that we had continued to stay friends on Facebook, and that when I needed help in the early days of starting my business, he was happy to lend a hand.

You don't have to be unkind just because your path is going in a different direction to someone else's. You don't need to burn the bridge that connects you.

Having great networking skills, or being great at making friends, doesn't have to come naturally. I'm an extremely judgemental person. I will happily, hand-on-heart, admit that the moment I meet someone I will make an immediate judgement about whether or not they should be in my life and in my circle. Then I'll take that judgement and put it to one side, because I know I'm a judgemental person.

At that point, I give someone two chances to prove me wrong. Most people invariably prove me wrong somewhere within those two chances. Which means that I very rarely burn bridges. Which is a good thing, because the minute you completely write someone off in your head, you're not just costing them money, you're costing yourself money. This is because you lose not only your relationship with that person, you also lose all the connections they have.

Of course, there are times when people write me off, because they have made a judgement. Often, this will relate to communication style. On the DISC profile I'm a very high D and a high I, which means that I don't do small talk. So if someone asks me to give them a *War and Peace* length speech about my family and what I did on the weekend, they're not going to get very far. It's not that I have no interest in talking to them. It's just that discussing my personal life is really not my style.

PUTTING IT INTO PRACTICE: EXAMPLE

Time-Delay Your Judgements

When I was at the BNI global convention in Warsaw in 2019, I met one of the executive directors. He was from the Netherlands. The working day had finished. It was four o' clock in the afternoon in Warsaw, which is pretty late at night in Australia, and I told him I was off to have a whisky. His response was to say, 'At this time of the day? You should be off to the hotel gym, not the hotel bar!'

I wasn't impressed, so I walked away thinking, 'Stuff you.' But I had to put that thought in a box, because I was in training with him for the next five days. And it turned out that he was a really nice bloke - the kind of guy who would move heaven and earth to help you. I now have somewhere to stay if I go to the Netherlands.

If I hadn't learned early on to reserve my judgements about people then I wouldn't have got very far. If I were really good at it, then I would have learned not to judge people in the first place. But I'm too set in my ways, so the best I can do is to put that judgement in a box, with a time-delay alert, and wait to see what happens.

Solving Other People's Problems

Going back to that very first invitation to a BNI meeting, although I could clearly see the benefits of becoming a member and quickly made the decision to join, I didn't know how to make everything work for me straight away.

What I was very clear about was that, in order to get the most out of my membership, I needed to solve other people's problems. Which is a very BNI attitude.

If I had spent my time running around chasing the other members asking if they needed help with their social media, then it wouldn't have worked. I figured that if I could help enough people, then at least some of those people would help me in return.

It was through helping others that I started building relationships. The person who had previously held the social media seat in that chapter had a 'burn and churn' mentality. So they were expecting another social media person with that approach to doing business. As a result, it took a little while to win everyone's trust.

The web designer, who I knew would be my major source of referrals in the chapter, rolled his eyes when the time came for us to have a one-to-one conversation. Even so, he bit the bullet and asked me to tell him all about myself. My response was to say that I was pretty boring, and that I'd like to hear about what he did, because web design was obviously pretty important to my clients. Then I said that before we got onto talking about web design, I'd be interested to know what floated his boat when he wasn't killing himself working an eighty-hour week.

I recognised that he was much more of an 'S' on the DISC profile, and so being asked about what he liked to do outside work was going to mean a lot to him. He would welcome the opportunity to talk about his hobbies and his family. Even if, as a high 'D', I would prefer to be talking business.

With a background in counselling, I had learnt to

become very good at reading people, which gave me the emotional intelligence to know when to shut up and listen, and when to let go of my own agendas when they clearly weren't aligned with those of the people I was talking to.

Engagement Creates Opportunity

After I had been a member of BNI for about three months there was director training being held in Wollongong, in New South Wales. Simon Derrick-Roberts posted the details of the training online, and I commented that it looked really cool, but that as I wasn't a director I wouldn't be able to go.

Little did I know that he was a brand-new franchise holder, and really needed directors. So he responded saying that although I wasn't a director, he would see if he could get the national director, Frederick Marcoux, to make an exception.

I thanked him, but I didn't really expect anything to come of it. Six hours later, he got back to me saying that I was allowed to come, and giving me the link to purchase my ticket. This led to a very awkward conversation with my husband at the time, because it meant I would be leaving him with two small children while I went off to director training for five days. But we worked everything out, and I headed over to Wollongong.

At that director training I met John Williamson, who was the executive director for Perth. We got stuck in the airport together on the way home. I was pretty much in overwhelm by this point, having well and truly drunk from the fire hydrant over the past five days.

Even so, while we were waiting for our flights, I mentioned that I'd been looking at BNI Australia's social media, and that it wasn't fabulous. I said that if there was ever an opportunity for me to have coffee with the person who was managing their social media, then I would be happy to give them some of my ideas.

He told me to leave it with him, and I didn't think any more of it. But having spent time with him at director training, and having had that conversation at the airport, it turned out he was now in my corner.

Fast-forward another year and a half down the

track, and Frederick, the national director, called me up. He said they'd really like me to look after BNI South Australia's social media, just to test it out and see how things went. He asked if it was something I would be interested in, and I said that it absolutely was.

From there, we began managing BNI South Australia's social media. After a year we were awarded the national contract. Throughout this time I had been going to director training with all the other executive directors, getting to know them better, finding out what was important to them, and helping wherever I could because making friends is good for business.

Taking No For An Answer

Not long after joining the director team for BNI SA, I met an amazing woman called Hazel Walker. It's her fault that I have a pub, and it's her fault that I have a BNI franchise. This is because I saw her give a presentation during which she told one of those stories you hear that changes the way you do things.

She had a sales coach who said to her that she

didn't like hearing the word no. She responded that she had no problem saying no. He pointed out that she had misunderstood, and that even if she was perfectly comfortable telling other people 'no', she didn't like it when people said no to her.

He set her a task. He told her that over the next week she had to get ten people to say no to her every day. And that for every day she didn't reach her target she had to give him $100, which he would donate to his political party. Which was not her political party.

So she started asking for things that seemed unreasonable, in order to get people to say no to her. On the first day she was doing quite well, until it came to the tenth 'no' that she needed for the day.

She asked the barista at her local coffee shop if she could get her latte free, and he said, 'Not a problem.' Taken aback, and slightly annoyed at being denied her 'no', she asked why. The barista explained that she was a nice lady and a good customer, that she'd never asked for anything before, so why not?

A couple of days later, she asked the double-glazing salesman who was quoting for new windows for her condo if she could get fifty percent off. He said no, but that he could give her thirty percent off. It seemed crazy!

She discovered that by asking for exactly what she wanted, more often than not, life would give it to her. And even if it didn't exactly pan out, she still got a pretty good deal.

When I heard her give this talk I decided to try it out. It seemed like reasonably sensible stuff. So I made a start.

PUTTING IT INTO PRACTICE: EXAMPLE

Know What You Want, Get What You Need

At events, when you are taking a table of clients, where you are in relation to the stage is a direct reflection of how important you are. You don't want to be in the nosebleed section at the back. There's a pretty good inference that if that's where you are, you're not that important.

I was taking two tables of clients to a Telstra function, where Hazel happened to be speaking.

I rang the event organiser and said I understood they would have the VIPs front and centre, but given that I had booked two tables, could I get front left or front right. They said that wouldn't be a problem. So I saw how the game was played.

Then, when I was looking for office space for the social media agency, asking for what I wanted meant that I ended up with a pub. I hired a broker and said that I was looking for a training room with natural light that could take about forty people. I said I needed a certain amount of office space, which could be upstairs if necessary. I said that I wanted a little bar or a café, because I was tired of paying for catering for all the networking events I was running.

His face was doing all kinds of weird stuff by this stage, and Tamara, my general manager, explained that it was ok, and she knew he wouldn't have exactly what I wanted, with the usual tone that implies I'm mad. He responded that this wasn't the case. He told us that he'd had a phone call an hour ago and he had what I wanted. It wasn't on the market yet, but would I be able to go and look at it with him at eleven o'clock that morning?

It just so happened that I could. Two hours later, I pulled up outside the Duke of Brunswick hotel. And a whole new chapter of my life began.

Letting People Be Human Beings

If you look at it from a networking perspective, one of the first things I did with the hotel was to launch two BNI chapters. This helped to keep the hotel profitable, as when I took over the Duke of Brunswick it was pretty run-down and in desperate need of being turned around.

Not only that, but one of the people I had met several years before at a Family Business Australia conference was a lawyer by day, and very involved in improvisational theatre in his free time. So he brought all his shows to the hotel, which meant that every Thursday night I had a good crowd.

I also made friends with the Bear Men of Adelaide, a social club for LGBTIQ bears. The Duke of

Brunswick had been their meeting place for a number of years, and they asked me the day after I took over the lease if they could still come and drink in the pub.

I still remember the conversation. They looked so concerned. I asked if they drank alcohol. They said yes, they did. I asked if there were lots of them. They said yes, there were. I questioned whether I needed to pay them or if they would pay me. They assured me that they would pay me. So the answer was that of course they were welcome! They were patrons like anybody else.

So it's really important to let people be human beings. I'm so happy to be able to say that I have an extremely diverse and wide network of human beings in my world.

Expanding The Circle

While I was building up the Duke of Brunswick, I was also building up a good relationship with Frederick, the national director of BNI. In 2017 I accompanied him to the global convention for BNI, as the marketing person for BNI Australia, and got a taste of what a global convention really looked like.

I asked him why we didn't have national conferences for BNI in Australia, and he said they had tried, but it had never worked. Undeterred, I encouraged him to give it another try.

I have now been involved with the Australian conference for BNI for the past three years. In 2021 it will be hosted in Adelaide, and we'll show them the true power of a networked town!

The simple truth is that the world keeps turning, and you make more and more friendships along the way. As a direct result of a presentation I gave at the Australian national conference in 2018, I was invited to speak at the global conference in Warsaw in 2019, which opened up more opportunities to make even more friends.

However, at no point is a decision made to make those friendships with the idea that they will help make my business profitable. I make those friendships because they are interesting humans in my network.

Paul Gordon, the lawyer, calls me The Oracle,

because if he ever needs a problem solved, he just picks up the phone and says, 'Who do you know that can do this?' The global network of BNI has made that even more powerful. Now I can help people in Turkey, Nigeria, Poland, the Netherlands, Peru, and so many other countries, because I've built those life-long relationships with those people at the global conventions over the last five years.

It's a really amazing world to live in when you know you have an extended family of people who will bend their will to help you reach your dreams. And the wonderful thing is that anyone can have it. They just have to be prepared to do the work.

Chapter One

The Unnatural Networker

If you've ever been trapped with a 'close talker' at a networking event, then you know why emotionally intelligent networking is so important.

The reality is that too many people have poor emotional intelligence. In other words, they don't have a filter. These are the people who are very fixed on their agenda, what they want to achieve, and what's important about them. However, successful business people are very good listeners, and they're very good at asking questions. These are essential skills if you want to build relationships.

Understanding emotional intelligence is not something that is taught in business school. We are not taught how to read body language. We are not taught what the person you are trying to engage with is doing that gives you an indication of whether you are getting things wrong in terms of your approach, or if you're on the money and you should continue on the same track.

PUTTING IT INTO PRACTICE: TOOLS

The Emotional Intelligence Health Check

A central part of networking is carrying out an emotional intelligence health check. Ask yourself:

• How emotionally aware of other people are you?

• Can you assess if the other person is interested or not interested in you?

• Can you read whether the person is keen on the topic you're talking about or whether they're trying to escape?

There are lots of different things you can do to increase your emotional intelligence. I recommend practicing on your partner, parents, and children. Children in particular are a great indicator, because they tend not to have filters and so they are easier to read. And, as parents, we put a lot more effort into reading our kids than into reading our peers. So practising with your kids (or your friends' kids) is a good way to carry out a health check.

Calculate The Interest Rate

The first point you want to consider is to ask yourself if you are talking about a topic that is of interest to the other person. Often, in networking, we'll go in hard with, 'What do you do for work?' If you've just had a massive day, then work may be the last thing you want to talk about.

Equally, if you're talking to someone who is a high 'D' on the DISC profile, asking what they did at the weekend will be a conversation killer. High 'Ds' don't like to talk about their personal lives with people they don't know.

A great way to get around this is to have a bank of questions in your back pocket, designed to get people's attention. I'll often still ask what someone does for a living as my opening question. This can then lead onto a question about what exactly their work involves.

PUTTING IT INTO PRACTICE: EXAMPLE

Asking Unexpected Questions

One conversation I had at a networking event was with a quality management auditor. Once I found out what he did, I asked what his work entailed. He explained that he went around auditing different companies to ensure their quality standards were up to par.

At this point, I was able to engage with him on a deeper level. I asked him to tell me about the most unusual company he had ever audited. This moved the conversation into much more interesting territory. His response was to tell me that no one had ever asked him that before!

He then went on to say he had audited a company that milked snakes for anti-venom. Which would have been fine for him, except he was terrified of snakes. At this point, the conversation became quite animated. I knew he would remember me because I asked him a question that he'd never been asked before.

More importantly, though, I was genuinely interested in the answer.

I was then able to build on the conversation from there. The whole time, I was paying attention to his body language, checking to see if he had open arms, if he was relaxed, or if he had one foot turned away, in 'escape pose'.

Reading The Signs

Alongside the body language signals listed in the example above, another really common scenario is to find that someone's eyes are scanning the room over the top of your head.

If you can't hold someone's eye contact then they've had enough. At this point, the smart networker politely sets them free, so they can have a conversation with someone else. Setting someone free is much better than burning the beginning of a relationship because someone feels trapped by you.

I'll often say something like, 'It's been really great talking to you, but I'm keen to catch up with someone, so if you don't mind, I'm going to keep looking for them. I'm more than happy to catch up with you at a later date, if you'd like.' If they then offer their business card, I am genuinely always happy to catch up.

Tuning In To The Signals

It's crucial to learn how to read the physical cues that signal changes in the emotional responses of the people you're networking with. If you are not able to do this, you're basically jeopardising the opportunity to form a meaningful relationship with that person.

The challenge is, the person you are talking to knows 150 other people, at least five of whom are probably your ideal clients. So everyone you meet matters. This means you need to be able to read people's cues, and build relationships over time.

I've seen people burn massive business deals, just because they couldn't work out that they were speaking to someone in a way that made the person feel talked down to. Or speaking to someone in a way that was so fixed on their own agenda that they didn't give the other person any air.

If it doesn't come naturally to you to leave space for

other people to breathe and be, what can you do?

I'm not a natural networker, which is why I call myself 'The Unnatural Networker'. It's not my default position to go out with people in large-scale groups, particularly in a networking environment. I'm much better in one-to-one situations.

I'm a terrible human in a lot of respects. It doesn't naturally occur to me to ask people about themselves. This is because if I want to talk about something, then I just talk about it. So I assume everybody does the same thing.

PUTTING IT INTO PRACTICE: TOOLS

Learning To Speak Human

If someone asks you how your day was, answer their question and then prompt yourself to ask them a question in return. You can create an internal cue that tells you, 'You've just answered a question.' This will then trigger you to ask them something from the list of questions that you have in your back pocket.

Back Pocket Questions

A few fairly common ones you can use, depending on what someone has asked you, are:

• *How has the week been panning out?* This is pretty generic, and something that you can lead in with.

• *What's been your biggest win this week?* This gives them the opportunity to talk about something they're happy about.

• *Have you hit any roadblocks this week that I can help you with?* This question is dependent on how good the relationship is with the other person. It is a good one to use if you have a reasonable relationship, and if you've already told them that you've hit a lot of roadblocks recently. It is good to ask how you might be able to help, because becoming someone who is known for being able to connect people with one another is often founded on thinking about how you can solve other people's problems.

• *How many events have you got on this week?*

Asking about the way in which they network is a natural way to move the conversation forward at a networking event.

PUTTING IT INTO PRACTICE: TECHNIQUE

Breathing Space

People are generally quite happy to chat to you if you just ask them normal questions. The important thing is not to be selling at people. You can start by introducing yourself.

You can then ask what they do. Even if they're wearing a badge that tells you. The badge might tell you that they're the CEO of an advertising agency, but you can still ask what their specialisation is. Then just keeping asking questions.

If they're interested in what you do, they'll ask. By not selling at them and telling them all about what you do and how you work with clients, unless they ask, you give them air. You give them the oxygen to breathe and feel comfortable.

Emotionally intelligent networking is also about maintaining space. Never get up in people's personal space. Half a metre between you and the other person is good. Basically, if you're not in their hug circle, that's probably a good thing. So if they can stretch their arms out without physically connecting with you, you're probably at the right distance.

Emotionally intelligent networking can be challenging in a lot of respects, but by finding cues that you can put in place which allow you to feel comfortable, you're most of the way there. This is because we sell at people when we're uncomfortable.

Don't Scare The Humans!

To a degree, you can treat networking events in the same way you treat social events. This doesn't mean drinking six tequilas at the bar. When you're networking, it's important to be careful with your alcohol and make sure you take it easy. But, as with social events, your job is to go in and make friends. *That is your one agenda.*

This is not a popular approach to take, as far as most networking gurus are concerned. If you read blogs on how to be an effective networker, they will advise you to have 'networking KPIs'. They will recommend that you contact the host before the event and ask for the attendee list. They will tell you to have a shortlist of three people you want the host to introduce you to at the event.

All of those blogs teach you how to be a hunter. In my view, hunters don't last very long in networking. The people in the world who are connected and have really solid networks and influence can spot these hunters a million miles away, and will mentally run for the hills when they see them coming. These highly effective networkers are generally emotionally intelligent enough to smile even while they're mentally high-tailing it, or as Dr Louise Mahler says, 'Nod, smile, and blink like an idiot.'

What she means by this is that when you are in your resting pose, if you stand with your arms relaxed, and just nod, smile, and blink, it makes you less scary to human beings.

So don't go hunting. If you want to be successful in life and actually build your network, it's not a short game. It's an extremely long game. You're networking for life. That's how it works. In being really clear about that, you will make business friends. You will need those business friends somewhere down the track. You may not know why or in what way, but it will come.

The story I tell in the introduction about buying the pub perfectly illustrates this. I had met a lawyer at a conference six years before and had vaguely kept in touch with him. It turned out he also happened to be the chair of an improvisational theatre group that needed a venue. Now he brings at least forty people into my pub on a weekly basis, and will do for the rest of time, as long as we don't upset them!

Because They're Worth It

People will come in and out of your life all the time. The key is to keep in mind that *a person always matters*. It's not about what they can offer you. They matter in and of themselves, because they're human beings. When you understand this, then you understand that every person is worth your time, and that your time is not more valuable than theirs.

One example of what this means is also one of my pet hates. This is people who arrive late to meetings with me. If people want me to spend money with them, arriving late is not going to go well. Generally speaking, I'm always ten to fifteen minutes early to every meeting. I'm happy to sit in someone's waiting room and read emails. In this day and age, it's not hard to keep working no matter where you are, so you're not losing any time by arriving early.

Another form this takes is people who are perpetually late, even if it's just two or three minutes. If you do this with someone who is always on time, or perpetually early, then they may not refer you to other people that could really help your business. This is because they are tying their reputation to yours. So their concern will be that if you are perpetually late, you'll make them look bad.

In the same way that being late can be damaging to your business, being early can help you in so many ways. For instance, it's much easier to read the room if you arrive early. If an event is starting at 5.30 pm, then I'll arrive at 5.00 pm.

PUTTING IT INTO PRACTICE: TECHNIQUE

Arriving Early

When you arrive early at a networking event, the first thing that it is helpful to do is have a chat with the event organiser. If it's someone you don't know, then take the time to get to know them. This also means you can give them a hand if they need any help getting anything set up, which is always nice.

As the other attendees begin to arrive, you're already there. It's much easier to have the conversations you want to have as the room builds up around you. It also means that if there are specific people you want to catch up with, then you can easily see where they are in the room, and who else there is in the room that you know. Essentially, arriving early to an event just makes it easier.

Another thing that you can do at networking events, from an emotional intelligence perspective, that helps to keep everyone calm and relaxed, is to sell somebody else in. If someone you know happens to be at an event you're attending, then if there's an opportunity, you can grab them and introduce them to somebody.

The introduction may run along the lines of, 'This is Craig, the graphic designer I was talking to you about, and you guys really need to go and have a coffee together outside of this event, because Adam is really not happy with his logo.' Selling someone in is really effective, because solving people's problems makes you the popular kid. And when it comes to networks that's what you want to be.

Getting Fluent In Speaking Human

One great way to be able to connect with people in a way that is going to be helpful in their lives is to talk to them about everything. Not just, 'How was your day?' When someone volunteers information about themselves, ask another question on that topic so that you move the conversation to a deeper level.

In doing this, you're going to open up a world of opportunities. In today's society, many people feel unseen, unheard, and unimportant. So if you meet someone at a networking event and make them feel like the most important person in the room, then you'll make their day.

This is a talent you want to cultivate in order to become great at networking. Think about how you can light people up. Can you tell the guy in the sharp suit which clearly cost a fortune that he looks great? Can you tell the woman with the bright green nail polish that her colour looks amazing? These are such little things, but they all play a part.

Pick Your Uniform

The above examples about how to light people up are both based on external appearance. However, you don't need to get dressed up in order to be a great networker. If wearing makeup feels unnatural to you, or you prefer to have loose, comfortable clothes rather than a formal suit, then that is absolutely fine.

It is true that people may make judgements about you based on your outward appearance, but there's a lot to be said for being unapologetically yourself. Within reason, of course.

Your outward appearance isn't the only thing people can make judgements about. It's not often that I'll walk into a room and not know at least a dozen people attending the event. Recently, though, I went to a networking event and, as I had been invited by one of their members, I only knew one person in the room, which was great! I love those rooms, because it means you've just found a whole new network to go and play in.

The person who had invited me mentioned to the event organiser that I had been impressed by the fact I didn't know anyone there. The organiser's response was to say that it wasn't surprising I didn't know anyone as I was in small business, and the people at the event had quite large businesses. This is a prime example of lacking emotional intelligence.

The upshot was that when the invitation came through for their next event, I decided I didn't really need to go and play. So knowing your audience is extremely important, as is not judging books by their covers.

Going back to your choice of uniform, there's something very wrong with the belief that someone's external appearance can make or break their success. However, it is true that there are a lot of judgemental people in the world. This means you've got to find the fine line. It's all about being yourself. If you are more comfortable dressing-down, then being clean, neat and presentable is all you need to aim for. Equally, if you like to dress up, then this is absolutely fine.

PUTTING IT INTO PRACTICE: EXAMPLE

Dress To Impress

Before Rilka Warbanoff, owner of Rilka's Real Food, started her own company, she was a really high-powered recruitment executive and would often go to events where she was the only woman.

Rilka has the most amazing 1950's dress sense. She always has fantastic outfits, her hair is always perfectly styled, and she has about twenty different pairs of beautiful eyeglasses.

She would turn up at the venue and be given a name badge, but she never wore it, she'd just put it in her purse. This meant that people would have to ask her name, and because Rilka is an unusual name it was easy for people to remember. So that was her way of being memorable.

Finding what works for you is key. Dressing up doesn't work for me, because I'm an introvert. If I choose to make myself the centre of attention, it's because I'm either really angry or really passionate about something. Otherwise, I'm happy to hold court in a small group. So understanding where your natural tendencies lie will allow you to be comfortable.

Key Takeaways

- Increasing your emotional intelligence helps you to build relationships.

- Instead of focusing on what the person you're speaking to can offer you, just focus on the person you're speaking to.

- You don't have to fake it to make it - be comfortable being yourself.

Chapter Two

Emotionally Intelligent Networking

The problem with networking events is that everyone is there to sell. No one is there to buy. The great majority of people are also not there to build relationships. This is why I love structured networking so much, and particularly BNI, because although everybody is there to find referrals, they are there to build relationships first. More importantly, they're not selling to the room, because BNI teaches its members not to sell to the room. There is nothing worse than being sold to when you are trying to build a relationship.

So if you're terrified of networking, structured networking groups, such as BNI, are great places to go in order to get used to the kinds of things you will encounter at networking events in an environment that is structured and safe, with thirty people who know how to build relationships.

BNI makes you a master networker over time. There's a lot of training that you're given about how to open network, how to have conversations with people, and how to break the ice. So the whole BNI experience allows you to feel very comfortable in a room, talking in front of other people.

When I first joined BNI I was terrified of my own shadow. The first time I had to stand up and deliver a referral request I was shaking. Over time, you become desensitised, and you build up immunity to the fear.

I'm not saying that BNI is for everybody. However, it was my path into becoming a good networker. There will certainly be resources available online that will get you up to speed. Or you can read this book!

PUTTING IT INTO PRACTICE: TOOLS

Keeping It Real

Whether or not you choose to join a structured networking group to build your confidence, there are still some simple cues that you can build for yourself to use in networking situations:

• *Am I speaking more than 40% of the time in a conversation?*

If that's the case, then it's probably time to exit the conversation.

• *Is the person selling at me?*

If this is the case, is there an opportunity to steer the conversation away from sales and towards neutral territory?

• *Did I make two new friends today?*

In terms of networking KPIs, this is the only one I have. If you can make two new friends at each networking event that you can go and have coffee with and learn more about their businesses and what they do when they're not at work, then this is great. Business can be lonely, isolating, and tiring, so the more friends you have in business, the less likely that is to be the case.

If you can ring someone from your network and ask about something you had been discussing with them a few months ago that now has relevance to your business, then they can help and support you. For example, if they were creating a new system for their employees that you are now looking to implement yourself, you can ask what the outcome was for them.

Top Tip!

Another advantage of having real conversations with people and collecting their stories is that you learn about different industries in a really in-depth way. This means that when you meet new people from those industries, you can talk to them in their language, which is really powerful. It's much quicker and easier to close a deal when you can talk to a financial planner in 'Plan Speak' rather than in 'Marketing Speak'.

How 'Real' Should I be?

Networking in real life is no different to how you run your social media. So on Facebook and Instagram, we don't post all the terrible things. On Instagram, you might take twenty-seven pictures in order to get that one perfect shot. Networking is pretty much the same. Judicious editing is required.

Although the aim of building a network is to form great, lifelong business relationships, and to be able to ask for help and advice from the people in your network, you do still need to put your best foot forward. Particularly in the early days.

PUTTING IT INTO PRACTICE: EXAMPLE

Picking Up The Reality Check

Telling someone you've just met that you've got an $80,000 tax bill and you don't know how you're going to pay it is not going to help build the relationship, or solve your tax problem.

On the other hand, telling them that you're facing a few challenges, but that you're really looking forward to branching into Allied Health may help you build the relationship, and if they know people in Allied Health who would be interested in working with you, it may also help you pay your tax bill.

If you really don't have anything positive to talk about, then that's probably a cue to go and get a business coach. Because it means that your lens is all wrong. And if your lens is all wrong and you're looking at all the negative stuff, then you're not going to dig your way out of that by turning up to a bunch of networking events.

If you find yourself stuck in a conversation with someone who is only focused on the negative, then escaping that conversation is important. Tell them that it sounds as though things are really rough for them, and that you know a really good business coach. Ask for their card, and let them know you'll make an email connection between them and the business coach. Then say goodbye.

You're still helping them, and that's what it's always about. Networking is a little bit like being an emergency room doctor. You do what you can to help, and then you move on to the next person.

Maximise Your Time

I'm a firm believer that, if you've booked a ticket for an event, then there will be someone there that you need to meet. On the rare occasion I decide not to go to an event that I've booked for, I'm always left wondering what opportunity I might have missed out on. There will always be at least one person you needed to meet, so it's important that you speak to as many people as possible, in order to find 'the one'.

Maximising your time doesn't mean going to endless events in order to meet as many people as possible. When my business was in the start-up phase, I had my weekly BNI meeting with forty or fifty people, and then I would try to attend one other event a week. So I had one event with my internal network, and one external.

PUTTING IT INTO PRACTICE: TECHNIQUE

The Strategic Networking Action Plan

Look at the three or four industries that have been referring you the most work. Then find out about their industry associations and how you can become a part of those associations.

One way to do this is to go and give a presentation to the members of the association, if you're comfortable speaking in front of people. If public speaking gives you the shakes then a good way to build confidence is to consider joining a group such as Toastmasters. Their weekly meet ups can be a great way to build both your skills and confidence.

If you don't feel ready to give presentations, then there may be 'member mixes' for people working in the industries you are interested in linking with, where you will have the opportunity to go and meet people. Alternatively, they may give presentations that you could attend, and mix with people from those industries.

Generally speaking, if you're looking to create links with industries outside the one you work in, there will be associate memberships available. For example, the South Australian Tourism Council offers professional membership to people in other industries. Social Media AOK is a professional member of the SA Tourism Council, which means that we can go and mix with all the tourism businesses, which is great, because they're our ideal clients.

As you go forward with networking, you can become more specific about the kinds of events that you're going to, and the kind of people you're meeting. You don't have to go to things that are advertised as networking events, and in fact it's probably better to avoid those kinds of things, or at least limit your attendance to once a month.

This is because these kinds of events often comprise start-up businesses and owner-operator businesses with small budgets. If those people are your target market, then that's fine and this type of networking event will clearly benefit you.

Understanding your target customer is important, but you then need to spider-web it out and keep on networking with new people to increase your circle of influence. There could be a tug on any of the threads.

PUTTING IT INTO PRACTICE: TECHNIQUE

How To Follow Up

Networking can happen anywhere. You could be on a training course, in a local bar, or grocery shopping. It doesn't matter where you are, you can still be networking and looking to make connections with people. But wherever you are, whether it's at a formal networking event, at an industry mixer, or in a pub, making the connections is only the first part. Once you've made a connection, you need to follow it up. And you need to follow it up in the right way.

The mistake that most people make is that they follow up the initial meeting by calling the person up and trying to make a sales appointment. As opposed to calling up and inviting the person to meet up in a way that strengthens the connection, without putting any weight of expectation on the relationship.

For example, you could call up and tell the person that it was great to meet them, and then let them know that you're hosting an informal lunch with twenty business owners in a couple of weeks time, and that you'd love to add them to the invite list if they're going to be free.

Again, it's about having a strategy for how you're going to build the relationship after that initial contact. It's so much more effective than either calling up to make a sales appointment, or waiting to speak to them at the next networking event in a month's time, where you might not remember each other anyway, because most people burn and churn at those events. Emotionally intelligent networking does not involve playing 'business-card poker' at networking events, where you just throw your card at people left, right, and centre.

No Need For Speed

Another big networking nightmare is speed networking. If I could make speed networking illegal then I would be so freakin' happy!

Speed networking helps nobody. It just makes everyone feel really awkward. Yes, it does force people to talk each other, but people rarely go back to conversations that are started during speed networking encounters. A few extroverts might enjoy it, but for the introverts, you might as well drag us across a floor of broken glass.

The truth is that most people like to choose who they network with, and take the time to get confortable with the person they're speaking to. If you give people sixty seconds on a clock, with the knowledge that a bell is going to go off at the end of that time, at which point they have to go and do it all over again with someone else, it is not going to help people build meaningful relationships.

Speed networking is also not helpful for those people who struggle with names and faces. However, there are always solutions to practical problems. I was taught a great trick by Frederick, the national director for BNI Australia, which he learned from John Howard, the former Australian Prime Minister.

PUTTING IT INTO PRACTICE: TECHNIQUE

Have We Met Before?

John Howard never said, 'Great to meet you.' He always said, 'Great to see you here.' He could have met you sixty times. He could have met you for the first time. Even just opening with, 'How are you?' is a great way to avoid the pitfall of not being sure if you've met someone before or not. You're still connecting with that person in a way that means something to them.

Knowing that you've met someone and not being able to remember their name can be tricky, especially when you know that you know them well enough that you should be able to remember their name. This is one reason why it can be really helpful to network with a wingman or wingwoman.

Taking someone along who is in an aligned industry, but not in direct competition with you, can be a great way to network. For a start, instead of selling yourself, you can sell each other. This is way better than banging on about how good your company is.

It also gives you the opportunity to avoid the awkwardness of not remembering someone's name. A subtle word to your networking partner, and they can either remind you, or jump in and introduce themselves and ask the other person their name.

In terms of filling any gaps in your emotional intelligence, having a partner is also really effective. You can learn from each other to improve your networking, so that you both become more confident and more effective.

Key Takeaways

- Find out how you can help the person you're talking to, then move on to the next person.

- Get specific about the events you attend so that you're networking with your ideal clients.

- Follow up on the connections you make at networking events – don't just play 'business card poker'.

Chapter Three

If You Don't Ask, You Don't Get

The first point worth making is that you can't ask for what you want if you don't know what you want.

In order to understand how powerful your networks are, you have to know how to use them, and how to access them. This starts with having clarity about what it is you're trying to achieve. As business owners, we often suck at this. We sit down at the start of the financial year and decide we would like to make a certain amount of money in sales, and save a certain amount of money in expenses, and those become the targets for what we want to achieve.

There might be some intelligence behind this in terms of the decisions we make about how much we spend on marketing, or the need to carry out a full expenses review. Generally speaking, though, I'll talk to most business owners who have told me that they want to make an extra 20% in sales, and ask what that looks like. They'll tell me it looks like a certain amount of dollars. Which is great, so then I ask how they're going to get that many dollars, and they'll tell me they need a certain number of new clients. I'll ask what type of clients, what industries those clients work in, who their most profitable clients are, how they are replicating that, how many of those people they already have in their network, and when they last spoke to them.

Inevitably, they haven't aligned their networking plan with their sales plan. They network because they're told that if you're in sales then you should network, and if you own a business you should network. The problem is, they haven't put any intelligence behind what it is they are actually trying to achieve.

PUTTING IT INTO PRACTICE: TOOLS

Creating Clarity

Creating clarity around what you really want to achieve is reasonably simple to do. The starting point is deciding that you want to make a certain amount more money. This then leads to working out how much more of a product or service you need to sell. Then, you can start to get really clear. This means working out:

- *Which industries are you most successful in?*

Work out the top three or four industries that bring you the most business.

- *Which clients are most profitable?*

These are the clients who pay a good price and don't chew up all of your time. You'll almost certainly find that 80% of those most profitable clients look and sound the same. They'll either fall within the same industry, they'll be the same age, or in roughly the same location. The answer to this question will lead you on to the next.

• *How do I get more of these clients?*

At this point, you can start to think of the people in your network who can help.

PUTTING IT INTO PRACTICE: EXAMPLE

Creating Clarity

Ted, an accountant I recently met, works with a lot of doctors. Social Media AOK has a really good track record in health, because doctors have a lot of APRA guidelines that they're held to, and we have a clear understanding of how to ensure allied health providers stay with in those guidelines.

I ask Ted what the opportunities would be for us to work with him, or to present to his clients on how to use social media in the face of the guidelines that they're bound by. Suppose that if we provided this service at no cost, would that be of interest?

As Ted is an accountant, the next step is to

think about what we can do to help him. Could we put on an event where Ted can speak about upcoming tax implications for a certain group of people?

When you know what you want, and what industries and customers you're trying to get to, then you can start to look at your network and see which people in your existing network fall into the right bucket, but are not your clients. Once you've found the 'right bucket' people, you can arrange to catch up for lunch with them. The other group of people that you want to look at are the people who are working with your existing clients. Who are your clients spending their money with, and how can you make friends with those people?

Once you have worked this out, you'll start to get a really clear picture of which other service providers or businesses you need to be friends with. And then, you can ask for what you want.

At this point, you can start to leverage your social media channels. If you've got really solid networks, then you can post on LinkedIn. You might say, 'LinkedIn family! I'm looking to take lunch with the top ten accountants in Adelaide. I want to pick their brains as to what the burning issues are for their clients when it comes to marketing, and what their concerns are.' In this way, you're not selling - you just want to learn.

Your LinkedIn connections will help you out. For a start, if they've got one of the top ten accountants then they'll want to let everybody know about it. They will also want their accountant to feel good, so they'll happily tag them in.

Set Your Intentions, Then Take Action

Business goals are a good place to start when it comes to knowing what you want. However, knowing what you want applies to everything.

Yesterday, I sat down with Tamara, my business manager, to go over our strategic plan. This plan has had multiple iterations over the years, but we were having a good laugh because some of the 2016 stuff said things like 'Find and acquire a *Seriously Social* business, maybe a bar or a café', which we did in

2018, and 'Buy or create a networking business' and I became a BNI franchise holder in 2019.

So I set my intentions to manifest those things four years ago. They say that a goal written down is one you'll achieve. Once I had written them down I then started taking action to put them into place. Some of that action would have been subconscious - I wouldn't even have realised the end goal I was moving towards, but after a while making the right decisions and taking the right paths starts to become second nature.

Once you've had some practice, you start getting really good at knowing what you want. And once you *know* what you want, you can *ask* for exactly what it is you want all the time. What's the worst that can happen? They say no. One way to greatly increase the chance of getting a positive response is to make sure you have enough in the favour bank to ask the question. That's the thing.

If I'm going to ask a best selling author that I met at a conference for five minutes if he can read my book and provide me with a testimonial, then I'm not going to get much luck out of that, let's be honest.

That author is probably getting paid A$20k to be at the event, and they don't know me from Adam. The reality is that it's still probably not going to stop me from asking. I might not expect a yes, but I might ask anyway. And in fact, I did ask Steve Farber to read my first book, *Seriously Social*. He didn't read it, but it was worth a shot.

This was around the same time that I asked Brian McDonnell from PayPal to read *Seriously Social*, and Jackie Booth from Zagame Corporation. They were both people I didn't know hugely well, and they were both quite happy to read it. So what would have happened if I hadn't asked the question? I definitely wouldn't have got any testimonials.

Stop Caring About The 'No'

A lot of people aren't great networkers because they're scared of the word 'no'. Essentially, they're scared of being rejected in some way. You're going to hear the word 'no' a lot in business. Not everybody says yes. Not every meeting turns into a client. Not every quote gets signed off on.

You've got to stop caring about the 'no' and start caring about the relationship. Make the relationship and the conversations that you have with people the most important things. This is the path to success.

It is also essential to ensure you have enough diversity in your network. This is because without diversity it's really hard to get 'yeses' or to get the right person to help you. So if you're a marketing person and you only know marketing people who are all selling the same product as you, it's pretty hard to get to where you want to be.

Whereas if you're a marketing person and you've got accountants, lawyers, financial planners, allied health practitioners, heads of hospitals, and all of these kinds of people in your network, and you've nurtured those relationships and spent enough time getting to know them and helping where you can, then you will have a really broad and robust network, and when the chips are down and you really need a favour you will have someone you can call who can connect you to the right person who can solve your problem.

PUTTING IT INTO PRACTICE: TECHNIQUE

Make Asking A Habit

They say it takes thirty days to break a habit or make a habit. So if you decide that you would like the world to start delivering you your manifestations then a really good way of speeding up that process is to spend thirty days trying to get ten people to say 'no' to you every day. Then just sit back and watch the world open up and deliver for you. The truth is that people don't actually want to say no.

If you think about it, people will say anything but 'no'. 'I'll have to think about it' is not 'no'. 'I need the run the budgets again' is not 'no'. They may want to say no, but they don't say no, because saying no is uncomfortable.

It is important to note that guilt-inducing a yes is not a win. Or bullying a yes. We've all met that person who always seems to get their own way, but everybody hates them. You don't want to be that person. Even if it brings you the trappings of success.

There's a new model for doing business that's built around community and 'win-win' relationships. It's all about how you can help the other person, with the knowledge that you're going to win somewhere down the track as a result. It's the BNI 'givers gain' philosophy. By helping someone else to achieve their dreams, at some point in the future they will help you to achieve yours.

This is where all the magical introductions come in. It happens to me all the time. I've had four Facebook messages today, all about menu enquiries for functions. It's all off the back of an article in the paper the other day, about how The Duke of Brunswick is a deaf-friendly venue. So now other people want to support us. It's got nothing to do with the deaf-friendly thing. It's simply in recognition of the fact that we're nice humans who are working really hard to be inclusive. I work hard to ensure we are inclusive because I feel great about myself when I do that. The win is that other people also feel great about it, and so they will help.

We need to shift the narrative. The old model of how to do business, which holds that 'nice guys finish last' is outdated. I'm a nice guy, and I'm not finishing last. I don't want to be the richest person in the room. I don't need to be. I would like to be the most joyful and grateful person in the room. I would like to have a great quality of life, and to be able to live my life the way I see fit. That's my definition of success.

By shifting your definition of success to how you made a difference today, the kindest thing you did today, and how you helped someone else achieve their dreams today, even if it was only to get them another inch closer, then you are working to the new model of how to do business. This way of thinking informs the kinds of questions that you are asking, and the way in which you ask for help.

PUTTING IT INTO PRACTICE: EXAMPLE

Defining Success

Ensuring The Duke of Brunswick is a deaf-friendly pub illustrates how this approach to business works. I informed Cathy, who was our functions manager at the time, that I wanted as many fringe acts booked in as humanly possible for the 2020

Adelaide Fringe Festival. To her credit, she secured ten acts and thirty-nine performances, which is huge for a tiny little pub.

I then decided to get all of the acts that would be performing together for lunch at the pub. Deaf Can Do, our partner for being a deaf-friendly pub, were invited as well. We already host their sip and sign events, and they've got various Auslan 'Learn to Sign' events happening around the Fringe.

Over the course of the lunch, Ali, the representative from Deaf Can Do, was talking about how much it cost to have an interpreter for the fringe shows. She explained that it was about A\$200 to A\$300 per show. I asked how we could get every single show interpreted. She said that the total cost would be about A\$20k, which would clearly be prohibitive.

I could see that all the fringe acts were getting very excited, so I asked if there was any way we could make it happen. Deaf Can Do then went to one of their corporate sponsors, The Flight Centre, and explained that we were really keen to have at least one performance of every act interpreted, which would total ten shows. This would be a first, so it would be a great marketing opportunity for everyone involved. The Flight Centre immediately agreed to pay. And that was as complicated as it got.

It's important to keep asking until you get to where you're trying to go. If I had given up when Ali said it would be cost prohibitive, then we wouldn't have been able to provide the inclusivity for our deaf patrons that we wanted to provide during the Fringe.

If you keep asking the same questions of the same people then you're not going to get anywhere. You need to ask different questions, and you need to ask different people. Again, this comes back to being good at asking questions, and always trusting that there has to be a way. So if there has to be a way, then by asking the right question of the right person, you'll get there eventually.

Asking, Asking, Always Multitasking!

Having become the first deaf-friendly pub in Adelaide, I'm now asking how we become the first veteran-friendly pub in Adelaide. There are so many returned service veterans with PTSD who often find social situations really difficult and stressful. We're already a dog-friendly pub, so we're great for assistance dogs, and so the next question is, 'Who do we need to talk to in order to start the journey to becoming a veteran-friendly pub?'

We're at the very beginning of that journey, so we don't know who to ask. A great place to start is Google. Starting conversations with the Jamie Larkin Centre, and Soldier On, and organisations like that means that we can start to find out how to run sensitivity training for the staff, so that they actually understand more about how to help, so that we have the capacity to provide a great space for our veterans.

Getting something that you've asked for doesn't need to be a stopping point. It means that you can then start looking around and seeing what else it is you want. You can have your goals right in front of you, and celebrate them when you achieve them, but it's important to look up every now and then and see what else will support you in enjoying what you do, having a great quality of life, and being able to do amazing things. This will help you to keep defining and refining who your markets are, who you want to be talking to, and what you want for yourself.

The Circle Holds Itself Together

The Australian Hotels Association demonstrates how this works across two of my businesses. The Duke of Brunswick holds membership to the association. Social Media AOK ran a series of training days for them last year, which they paid for. And this year, when I was putting on a social media trends workshop, the membership manager, who was on our email database, received the email about the workshop and asked if she could forward it to all their members. The answer was, of course, yes!

So now, whenever we are running a workshop, we offer a discount to all Australian Hotels Association members, and their membership manager emails all their members to invite them to the workshop. Their database is much more powerful than mine, so this is great for me.

This is not only an example of how two of my businesses support each other; it's also an example of why you need to keep networking out. Unless you're an employee who has no plans to move beyond the role that you're in, and your role isn't sales, then it's no good if you have a network of just forty people. When you keep networking out and an opportunity presents itself, then you can look for what other opportunities are around it.

PUTTING IT INTO PRACTICE: EXAMPLE

Networking Out

Years ago, one of the organisers of the first big social media conference to be held in Canberra was on Twitter tweeting about the event. I tweeted back and asked if he was looking for speakers. And he was. I said that if he paid for my flights and accommodation then I'd come and play. So he said ok.

I flew over to Canberra, where one of my business associates was working as a staffer for a federal member of parliament. After the conference opener, my associate took me on a behind-the-scenes tour of Parliament House. I sat in for question time, then went back and did my speaking gig at the conference that evening.

After the conference, I texted my business associate to thank him for taking me round Parliament House, and said I hoped he was having a nice evening. He told me that he was at the Press Club for an Australian Parliamentary Friends of the Rugby event. He asked me if I'd like to meet him there, to watch The State of Origin.

And so I went to the Press Club to watch The State of Origin, with all the federal members of parliament drinking their beer. Which was a good problem to have.

It all stems from having taken action. One initial question, about whether the social media conference needed speakers, led to that entire series of events.

The More Questions You Ask, The Bigger Things Get

Asking for what you want gives you things to look forward to. Because once you get into the habit of asking for what you want, you start to ask other people what they want. When you do this, they start telling you what their hopes and dreams are, which ignites a fire in them, because they can talk about what they're passionate about.

If you're able to help people, even just a little bit, with fulfilling their dreams, then this ignites a fire in you. At which point it becomes less about business, and more about helping people.

I always said that my one burning desire was to make myself redundant, to a point where my only job was to attend breakfasts, lunches, and dinners, and speak to people. I'm pretty much there. This is essentially what my job is these days. So once you know what you want, you can set about making it happen. And how you do that is to ask people what, why, and how.

Key Takeaways

- Create clarity around what you want - if you don't know what you're working for then how can people to help you achieve your goals?

- Shift your definition of success from how much you can get to how much you can give.

- Getting something you've asked for doesn't need to be a stopping point. Instead, it can be an opportunity to celebrate, before looking around to see what else you want.

Chapter Four

Taking Calculated Risks

A network is no good to you if you don't leverage it. Interestingly, lots of people think that they have really good networks until they try to leverage them, and then they discover that they don't have networks at all. They just have collections of people's phone numbers.

Leveraging a network, or as Ivan Misner likes to say, 'Networking Up' or 'Networking Sideways' involves doing some maths. You need to have a fairly clear understanding of what your relationship is with each person in your network, how many points you have on the board in terms of how often you've helped them, how close you are to them, and how well you know them.

Funnily enough, people often fail to do the maths.

They then get to a point where they're desperate. For instance, they might really need to fill a course or an event, and it goes from them being very pleasant about it with their marketing to pleading requests for people in their network to send out invitations to people in their databases or to call ten people and tell them to come along. This is a common one, but generally, networking maths is all about asking for a favour, regardless of what that favour might be.

PUTTING IT INTO PRACTICE: EXAMPLE

Getting The Maths Right

The value of the favour that you're asking has a direct correlation to how much credit you need to have in the favour bank.

Let's take the example of Ivan Misner writing the foreword for my first book, *Seriously Social*. I did the mental arithmetic and concluded I didn't have enough credit in the favour bank to ask Ivan personally, because I didn't know him well enough. I've met him a few times and I have his contact details, which is fantastic, but it doesn't make us friends. So I went to the person I knew who was closest to Ivan, and who I had enough credit in the favour bank with, and asked him to ask Ivan.

You take calculated risks with your networks all the time. The big mistake that people make is that they don't evaluate their networks to work out whether they're helping them get to where they want to be in life. So they stay in networks that they shouldn't, and ignore networks that they should be actively participating in.

PUTTING IT INTO PRACTICE: EXAMPLE

Getting To Where You Want To Go

There are currently no BNI chapters in the north of South Australia, so we need to grow a lot of them. I'm in the middle of starting a chapter in Gawler, and we also want to launch a new chapter in Salisbury.

My first step was to work out where all the

networks are in and around Gawler and Salisbury. I then thought about who I know who lives and works out there, and who I should be catching up with.

Taking Salisbury as an example. I have two clients out there, but I don't go out there and actively network as I tend to network in the city, which is close to my office.

However, because I am looking to launch a BNI chapter in Salisbury, I went to a networking event specifically because it was in Salisbury. Funnily enough, the economic development officer for Salisbury was attending the function. So I got to have a really good conversation with him. The next step will be to go and have a coffee with him, to develop the relationship and start the conversation about launching a BNI chapter in Salisbury.

To a degree, you have to pay the piper. Sometimes you get to the end of the working day at 4.30pm, you've got a networking event at 5.30pm, and you have to drive for 40 minutes to get there. It's the last thing in the world that you want to do. You can almost taste the glass of wine. Not the one at the networking event. The one from your fridge, when you're at home in your tracksuit pants, relaxing.

However, the opportunity you lose by not turning up to an event you've booked a ticket for is an opportunity you'll never get back. There will always be someone that is the next step to somewhere you want to go.

PUTTING IT INTO PRACTICE: TECHNIQUE

Mapping Out Your Life

Start with your business goals. What are you trying to achieve? Think very carefully about what you need to look at.

Is there a geographical component? Do you need to be better known in a certain area? In this case, the next step is to think about what networking events and meet up groups are in that geographic area, so that you can attend them and start the conversations you need to have.

If it's industry-based, rather than geographical, the next step is to think about which industry associations your ideal clients and referral partners are playing in, so that you can join them.

It's always a risk meeting new people. Some people will leap into a room full of other people. Others will be standing back trying to figure out if there's just one single other human being to speak to. It's very much about having the courage to be yourself. If we go back to emotional intelligence, then making sure you are prepared, that you arrive early, and that you feel comfortable in your surroundings, is all really helpful.

It is also a good idea to nurse one drink throughout the evening, rather than having six. If you're feeling unsure of yourself, there is always a temptation to hit the bar. The same thing is true if you're a bit tired. It's easy to prop yourself up with a couple of extra glasses of wine: easy but not usually wise.

PUTTING IT INTO PRACTICE: EXERCISE

Think Like A Chess Player

The saying *'Fortune favours the brave'* exists
for a reason. There is a lot of strategy behind
networking. You need to know what the moves
are that you want to make. You might not know
where you're going to end up in six moves' time,
but you know where you want to end up. This means
that, at the very minimum, you know the first
move you need to make.

So roadmapping is very important, and being
very clear about the questions you need to ask
yourself. It always starts with your business. Plan
the first move and the end result. Everything in
between is left open, because it's contingent on
other people. Just like chess, where you move your
piece will dictate what possibilities open up and
where you go next.

In going out to the networking event in
Salisbury, I know this needs to be my first move
in order to reach the end result of having a BNI

chapter in Salisbury. But I don't know who is going to be there, and so there's no point in trying to plan the next move until I have attended the event. I made the calculation that I needed to go to the event, but from there, everything was open.

In fact, at that event, as well as meeting the economic development officer for the region, I was asked to present a workshop on social media to the business enterprise centre out there, which will put me in front of twenty or thirty business owners who may be interested in joining the BNI chapter. I also ran into the former business advisor for the area, who has heaps of connections. This means that I now have multiple games of chess happening at once, all working towards the same outcome.

PUTTING IT INTO PRACTICE: EXAMPLE

Analysis Paralysis

When you try to plan in too much detail it can feel overwhelming and stop you from being able to make that first move. This is something that I am aware can happen to me.

One solution I have found is that I never look at my diary for the entire week, other than once on a Friday. By 11am on a Friday, my diary is locked for the following week. No more appointments are allowed to go in after that time. So after 11am, I'll spend ten minutes seeing what my week looks like, and then I don't look at it from that point of view again. I'll open it each morning, and look at what I have on that day, and work out what I need to prepare for. Otherwise I would get overwhelmed and be incapable of doing anything, because I'd be too stressed.

If you try and look at the whole equation as one massive blackboard that's covered in endless numbers and symbols, you're never going to solve anything.

You need to approach things one little bit at a time.

It's like a first date. You have to start by asking someone. If they say yes, you then have to think about where you're going to take them, what you're going to do, what day you're going to do it on, and what you're going to wear. If you've already planned everything out all the way to walking down the aisle before you've even met somebody, then you'll break it. Not only will it be overwhelming to try and put it into practise, but you'll have your own agenda.

We've all been trapped with the person who is only interested in the sale. All they can see is the dollar sign above your head, and that's all that you are. It doesn't work. Sometimes those people will get sales, because they just keep burning bridges until they get what they want. But taking calculated risks does not mean marching up to someone and telling them to buy from you.

Becoming The Connector

Effective networking is a long game, and building a network where you're the centre of influence is a very long game. We love those people in their fifties and sixties, the ones that everyone knows and gravitates towards because they're the connectors. They have reached this point because in their thirties and forties, and even now in their fifties and sixties, they understand that it's not about what a person can do for them, it's simply that there is a person in front of them that they can get to know.

When you approach everything from the standpoint of thinking about how you can help the other person, then you will build networks. So the other calculated risk that you can take with every person you meet is to apply the belief that if you help enough people and are always in the habit of asking for what you want, then eventually the two things will meet.

This is how it works, as opposed to asking enough people to buy from you in the hope of eventually getting someone to say yes, no matter how many relationships you have burnt in the process.

Key Takeaways

• Networks are of no use unless you know how to leverage them.

• Plan the first move and the end result. This enables you to take action without becoming overwhelmed or getting fixed on your agenda.

• Help other people and keep asking for what you want to create strong, supportive networks that will last a lifetime.

Chapter Five

Moving To A Bigger Pond

Most people went to school. School is a very little pond in comparison to the world around you. In that little pond, particularly in your class, everybody knows you. They know your story and they know what you're about. There are two really interesting things about this.

The first is that once people know what you're about, then to a great extent you are forced to keep playing that game and being that person. You might be the sporty kid or the kid who's good at maths or the popular kid. The second is that if you change schools, for example when you go from primary school to high school, then you are suddenly given the license to completely reinvent yourself.

You also meet people who teach you new things,

and this allows you to continue to grow and develop. There is a saying that you are the sum total of the five people you spend the most time with. To an extent, I believe this is true. To expand on that idea, there is also a danger that you are a sum total of the networks you play in, or the ponds you swim in.

Be A Social Chameleon

The people who are successful in life are very careful not to be social dopes. They tend to be very culturally aware, with a great sensitivity to divergent cultures. They also tend to be aware of different industries and the stresses placed on those industries. Above all, the most successful networkers can change and adapt their communication style and their language and sentence structure to fit the room that they're in. They are social chameleons. This ability stems, in part, from having a really high degree of emotional intelligence.

PUTTING IT INTO PRACTICE: EXAMPLE

Moving On Up

Once I'd had Social Media AOK for two and a half to three years we were doing reasonably well. I probably could have trod water in my safe little pond at that point and had a comfortable life.

We had very established networks. I was a member of a BNI chapter and was quite well known as a director consultant. Alongside BNI, we were a member of the Eastside Business Enterprise Centre, which was a bit like a Chamber of Commerce. So I was reasonably well known in these two networks, we had an adequate amount of work coming in, and I could have stopped there. Lots of people do.

The problem with that, though, is that I wanted to continue to learn and expand. I wanted to meet new people and have interesting conversations so that I could learn from them. My favourite saying is 'No coffee is ever a waste of time'. I like to have new coffees with new people, all the time.

The way to go about doing this is to ask yourself which network you need to be a part of next. Google is your friend here. All you need to do is start Googling 'Business Networking' and 'Industry Associations'.

So when I decided I needed to make my pond bigger, the next organisation I came across was Brand South Australia, which has since been defunded, closed down, and taken over by Showcase SA. However, at the time it was Brand SA.

What happened with Brand SA was that their social media person left to go and work with the RAA. She's a very good public relations person, and it was the right move for her. But it meant that Brand SA needed a new social media trainer, and she put me forward. I had a meeting and asked them to talk to me about their network. They explained that they had 500 members, small, medium, and large organisations across twenty different sectors, all with businesses based in South Australia.

I asked if they would like me to take on a membership and provide four professional development sessions a year for their members. They said yes. It seemed like a good plan. Because I was effectively being given license to demonstrate my expertise to my target market, which is business owners, managers, and CEOs.

In the first year of working with Brand SA, did this opportunity turn into money raining from the sky? No, it didn't. Because you have to take time to form relationships. What it did do was to position me as an expert, which enabled me to continue building my brand in the South Australian business community.

I took that role for three years. Two years into my role with Brand SA, when I was quite well-established in that network, I began looking for the next network. I found the South Australian Tourism Industry Council, a membership organisation for tourism operators. We've now been associated with them for two years, doing exactly the same thing that we did with Brand SA.

Not everyone can get up on stage and train or talk. I'm not suggesting you should go off and become a public speaker. It's not everyone's cup of tea. What you can do, though, is go and take on an associate membership with an organisation.

So if you want to work with financial planners, take an associate membership with the Financial Planning Industry Association. Have a look at what inter-industry mixers the Chartered Accountants Association does, or the Medical Professionals Association.

You need to do this, because you need to walk into rooms where you don't know anyone. If you're walking into rooms where you know 80% of the people, then although this is lovely, generally speaking, it is also way more of a social situation than a business situation. More than this, those people are already going to refer you.

When you start noticing that you know the majority of people at an event, it's time to look for new events. My mantra is that I want to work so hard that I get to a point where I can walk into a room and not need to introduce myself. That is about serious personal brand clout. Not just choosing one room and staying in it until everybody knows me.

People feel safe and comfortable in a smaller pond. You know how everything works in a smaller pond. So for the unnatural networker moving to a different pond can be terrifying.

Walking into a room where you don't know more than one or two people means that you have to talk to people you don't know. You have to play the game and flex your networking muscles by asking interesting questions and carrying on conversations. But when you do this, you make really good connections, and you don't know where those relationships will go.

I'm still stunned that someone I met four years ago is now the economic development officer in an area where I am starting a BNI chapter. They weren't in that role when I met them. Now, they are really critical to my business - and that relationship is critical to my business. When we met four years ago we were just making friends and having coffee.

It's a variation on the idea that a stranger is just a friend you haven't met. In the context of networking, a stranger is just a connection you haven't made.

PUTTING IT INTO PRACTICE: TECHNIQUE

Doing The Work

Once you've made a connection you have to do the work. There are some really simple mechanics for how this works.

If you've just met someone at a networking event, go and find them on LinkedIn. Send them a connection request and a message saying that it was great to meet them at the event, and that you hope to catch them at another event soon. That's it. Do not send them a two-page essay.

Once they've accepted your request, they can see your content. This means that you're starting a conversation. If you're particularly interested in them, and think there's potential to work together, then go and find their business page on Facebook and like that. You can then comment on some of the things they are talking about from time to time.

The next step is to find another event that is close to where they live or work, and invite them to go with you. Alternatively, let them know that you're going to be in their area in two weeks' time, and ask if they'd like to meet up. Once you've made the connection, in order to expand your pond, you need to empower your networks.

So how do you make sure you're doing everything you need in your business and continuing to expand your network?

PUTTING IT INTO PRACTICE: TECHNIQUE

Systematic For The People

Doing everything you need to do in your business and continuing to expand your network is about having a system. If you have a system, then it's not actually that difficult.

If you know that 9am to 9.20am on a Tuesday is your networking follow-up time when you send all your messages and emails to your contacts, and it's in your diary every week, then that's easy.

Once a month, have an hour where you work out which networking events you will be attending the following month, then book your tickets and put the dates in your diary.

There are two different versions of networking. There's networking on steroids, which involves attending one external networking event a week. Alternatively, if you're just dipping your toe in, then one external networking event a month is fine. And if you're serious about growing your business then go and find a BNI chapter, and go to that once a week.

BNI is structured networking, as opposed to unstructured networking. Unnatural networkers are naturally comfortable in a structured networking environment, because all you have to do is work through the agenda. But you need to do both in business. You need to have some form of structured networking, and some unstructured networking.

Other versions of networking are forum groups and business mastermind classes. It's all still structured. You're meeting the same people every week or every month. You have a facilitator and you have open discussions and get to know people better, but it's all in a controlled environment, unlike a Chamber of Commerce event or an industry mixer.

It is still important to attend unstructured networking events. The main drawback with these types of events is that everyone is there to sell and no one is there to buy. As a result, many people give up after they have only been to a handful of these events. But these types of events are the ones that take a couple of years before you get any real benefit.

For example, with Chamber of Commerce events, you need to be going to their events regularly, maybe once a quarter. You don't need to go every month, as you always need to weigh up the time cost-versus-benefit with these things. But going along once a quarter, seeing who you meet, and then making sure you follow up, is a good strategy. Invite the people you connect with for coffee. Engage with them online. Don't just wait to see them at the next Chamber of Commerce event and hope to build a relationship like that.

Once again, it's about having a process that sits behind it. When you meet someone at an unstructured networking event and you have no contact with them until the next event, you can't expect to have formed a closer relationship with them. You might be latching onto each other like limpets, because you're the only person the other one knows, even if you only know each other from these events. However, that isn't the same as having a relationship.

Unstructured networking events, such as Chamber of Commerce events, are great for beginning conversations. After that, you have to put the work in to create deeper conversations afterwards.

PUTTING IT INTO PRACTICE: EXAMPLE

Laying The Groundwork

Justin works for an IT company doing extremely complex software integration work. I met him at an unstructured networking event, and then followed this up with coffee. We had a chat about each other's businesses, and then that was that. Until about a year later, when he called me up to ask for my help.

His company had a really complex piece of software that solved a particular problem for an aged care facility, and had saved the facility A$1.2 million. However, they didn't know how to explain what they had done on social media. They just couldn't make it translate, because it was too technical. So he asked if I could go and have a meeting with the company and simplify everything.

We had a meeting and talked everything through. I referred them to a graphic designer who was great at creating infographics. We mapped out exactly what the key points were that needed to be covered, and the graphic designer got to work. Meanwhile, we created the strategy around how they could roll this out across their channels and get it in front of the right people.

This was a fantastic job, and it came about because I moved a meeting at an informal networking event to the next stage, by going for coffee and finding out more about Justin's work.

It's always about nurturing the relationship. It's important to remember that the coffee is not about selling - it's about finding out more about the other person, without making judgements or assumptions.

PUTTING IT INTO PRACTICE: EXERCISE

You're Not The Most Important Person

Judgements and assumptions get in the way of making money. You can form an opinion once you've listened, and listened, and listened some more, and then asked questions so that the other person can clarify things for you. At that point, you may choose to volunteer some information which may be of assistance to them, but only after you've asked permission and they have assented.

Even then, it's a good idea not to tell people what you think. Instead, tell people *what your experience has been*. If you don't have personal experience then you could tell them what worked for someone you know who has been in a similar situation. When you're making friends, *it's not about you.*

It isn't always easy to keep the focus off yourself. If you're a talker, it's a good idea to frequently health check whether you're talking too much, and whether you're using the words 'I' and 'me' a lot. If so, you need to change the narrative.

Another point that you need to watch out for is to make sure you're not 'one-upping' the other person. If you ask someone about something they did, only to then say that you did the same thing, but you did it while jumping out of a plane with no parachute, it's not going to help the relationship. It's a misguided attempt at making a connection and impressing the other person all at the same time. Instead of validating what the other person is saying, though, it just hijacks the conversation.

The other thing to be careful of is defaulting to where you're comfortable. Something I am guilty of is defaulting to talking about business. I will happily tell people about the latest A$50k deal that we've just signed. My partner Alex gave me some great feedback when he told me that some people find talking about money and business deals off-putting.

I hadn't even recognised it, but then I began to see there was a pattern. When I was feeling unsure in a situation where I hadn't met someone before, I would begin to talk about how successful my businesses are. It's very obnoxious behaviour, and I was grateful to Alex for pointing it out, as it means I have been able to stop doing it.

Softly, Softly

When you're networking, particularly in one-to-one situations, you're not the most important person. Not if you want to have successful relationships. The person you're talking to is the most important person, and so you need to defer to them.

This is an obvious sales technique, and if you do it well, networking and selling are the same. Relationship-based sales techniques and networking occupy the same space. As with any relationship, taking things slowly is the way to build a deeper connection. Telling them how great you are is not going to make you more attractive - in fact, quite the opposite. You earn more credibility by asking really intelligent, probing questions, and then responding to the person's answers after you've listened to what they have to say.

When you're networking with very successful people, it's good to remember that they get asked a lot of the same questions, and many of those questions don't have a lot of thought behind them. So if you can be the intelligent person that asks the interesting questions and then responds to their answers, you will stand out and they will remember you. Then, when you want to go for a coffee, the chances are that they will say yes, because they know they can have a great conversation with you.

Key Takeaways

- Adapt how you communicate to suit your audience

- Create a system to expand your network, including both structured and unstructured events in your diary.

- Take the time to find out more about the people you're building relationships with - free from judgements or assumptions.

Chapter Six

Personality Types

Before thinking about anybody else's personality type, it is important to understand your own. If you don't know your personality type then there are many different tests available. My personal favourite, and the one I find easiest to understand and to explain is DISC profiling. There are numerous free online DISC profiling tests that you can use which will give you a rough idea of your personality type.

You may also want to do advanced DISC profiling, which will give you much more detail and is far more helpful. When you're in a high level corporate position it's important to understand how you operate, so that you can help facilitate your team management.

Overall, though, DISC profiling is reasonably simple. Generally people will have two dominant traits on their profile, with the other two forming a far less intrinsic part of their personality. For example, I am a high 'D' and a high 'I', fifty-fifty split. I have very little 'C' and very little 'S' in my personality.

PUTTING IT INTO PRACTICE: EXAMPLE

DISC Profiling

As a dominant personality type, I'm interested in talking about business. I also need you to give me answers very quickly and succinctly. I need you to tell me why I need to pay attention to you, what I need to pay attention to you for, and what's in it for me. This makes me a very unnatural networker. If high 'D's can't adapt their style, they can come off as really aggressive, arrogant, argumentative, and confrontational. These are all the downsides.

My other dominant trait is the high 'I', which is the influencer. I like bright shiny objects. So I'm very easily distracted. I like exciting stories about business, and if I meet you once at an event I'll assume we're friends. Then if I meet someone else at another event, I'll tell them that they have to go and talk to you, that you're the most amazing human being, and that you've done all kinds of brilliant things in your business.

Being a high 'D' and a high 'I' creates the perfect marriage of business and enthusiasm for me. However, high 'I's also tend to be namedroppers. We like to talk about who we've worked with and we focus on the exciting things. Once again, you have to work to hold our attention. So if I meet someone who is a 'C' type, a methodical, research-based personality, they are going to go into a lot of detail, and I'm going to get bored really, really quickly. As a result, I have to mentally make a note that I need to pay attention.

Likewise, with the 'S' type personalities. They're going to ask me what I did on the weekend. I don't care what I did on the weekend. The weekend is over there, in the box marked 'personal'. But they care. They also want me to ask them what they did on the weekend. They want to find out if I've got kids and to know if I've got anything planned for the school holidays. All of this is in the context of a business networking meeting, but I will make small talk, because that's what's important to an 'S' type. They're all about relationships.

In the same way that we've talked about the importance of emotional intelligence when it comes to reading people's body language, and whether you have their attention or not, when it comes to personality types, you need to get really clued up on working out what personality type the person standing in front of you is presenting you with. Once you can do this, then you can adapt your communication style to suit the person you are talking to.

It's about making sure the other person is comfortable. If you're a good networker, you'll change the way that you speak, you'll change the tone you use, and you'll change your body language to fit the person you are talking to.

Of course, this is fine if you're in a one-to-one situation, but what do you do if you're in a group with a mixture of high 'D's, high 'I's, high 'C's and high 'S's?

This is a good challenge to have (because we never have problems, only challenges!). Often, you will naturally gravitate to the person who is the same as you. But there are all sorts of interesting things that can happen in that scenario.

PUTTING IT INTO PRACTICE: TECHNIQUE

Becoming The Glue

If you're a high 'D', and there's another high 'D' in that group then you will both want to hold court. As will the high 'I's. If you're not careful, you will end up having a competition about which one of you is the most successful and interesting person. We've all seen that conversation playing out. While it is happening the 'C' type personality will be mentally taking notes, but won't say much or volunteer their views.

Once you know that this is what's happening,

you can say to the high 'D' that they have made some really interesting points, and then turn to the high 'C' and ask them what their experience of this has been in their industry. Pick up a key point that is data driven or technical, so that it is detail-oriented, and ask them their opinion.

'C' type personalities won't tend to offer their opinion until they have done all the research and have all the facts, but if you ask them what their experience is then they will be happy to speak about what they know.

The 'S' type personalities can be included by steering the conversation towards something they enjoy doing outside work, preferably in a way that relates to the points that have been made by the 'D's, the 'I's and the 'C's. So if, for example, a high 'D' has been talking about a business trip he is due to go on to China, then you could tell the high 'S' that you've been thinking about taking a course in Chinese cookery, and ask if they have any hobbies or interests.

The successful networker will bring all of the different personality types together. You become the glue. You need to be aware of whose voice hasn't been heard, and whose voice you're hearing all the time. You can tell the person who is dominating the group that what they're saying is really interesting, and then you can steer things to someone who hasn't said much, and give them some airtime.

If you're the person that's giving everyone airtime, and engaging them, and weaving conversations together, then you're the person that will be memorable. A good networker makes sure that everyone gets time in the spotlight. At the same time, they understand that some people, based on their personality type, will be less comfortable in that spotlight. So being a good networker means recognising other people's needs, and finding a way to meet them.

PUTTING IT INTO PRACTICE: EXAMPLE

Fixing Mistakes

A close friend of mine is an executive director, a very successful woman, but an 'S' type personality, so not always one to put herself forward. We were at the global conference for BNI in Warsaw, and she was due to get her five-year director pin. It's a big deal. It shows a high level of commitment to the organisation, and when you receive the pin it is handed to you by the chief operating officer of BNI.

Unfortunately, you have to send through the nominations for a five-year pin ahead of time. There had been an oversight, and it hadn't been picked up that she was due for her pin, so the nomination hadn't been sent through.

When she enquired about her pin, the response she got from the person she spoke to was that nothing could be done. As an 'S' type personality she wasn't going to make a big deal out of this, because that's not what 'S' types do. Instead, they get sad. Very sad.

I knew it was a big deal for her, so I spoke to the person myself, quietly, not in front of my friend, and explained that it was the first time my friend had been to a global BNI convention, and that it was the first time she had been overseas. More than this, she was involved in an organisation where recognition is very important. So who could we speak to in order to fix the oversight and make sure she got her pin?

I was sure there had to be a way. And there was. To his credit, the person responsible went and fixed it, and she got her pin. Not only was this a situation in which I was able to ensure my friend's needs were met, it also provided an opportunity for the person responsible to fix a mistake. Picking up that someone has burnt or harmed a relationship inadvertently, and having the skill to give feedback in the manner that they can hear based on their personality profile, gives them a chance to fix the relationship.

If you can fill in the gaps, in group situations and with individuals, then you will be able to consider yourself a highly skilled networker. Your voice doesn't need to be the loudest in the room. In fact, if you watch people who are really good at networking, then apart from an enthusiastic 'hello!', with hugs and cheek kisses, they are never the loudest in the room.

Oh So Quiet...

The people who wield real influence in their networks are never the loudest. Often, they can be overlooked. When you walk into a room to network, see if you can figure out who the real powerbrokers are. It's not the person up on stage all the time - it's really not. It's often the person who is going round making sure everyone is comfortable and has someone to talk to.

No one expects you to be able to take this role straight away. Networking can take a certain degree of bravado in the beginning, especially if you are uncomfortable with people, as I am. You wouldn't know it externally, but internally, I have all the usual fears about being liked by people I don't know. And yet I walk into rooms filled with people I don't know on a regular basis. This is why I've developed all these tricks to make it easier.

Being able to connect people to one another, so that they can hear each other, is one of these tricks. Keeping everyone involved in the conversation does mean that you have to be fairly well read on a wide variety of topics. There will always be gaps in your knowledge, and sometimes you need to be good at bluffing. For instance, I don't watch the news, so I have to be careful with how I choose my words in order to stay involved in the conversation. Asking questions is a good way round this.

Driven To Succeed

Networking is a skill that you learn over time. It is not unlike learning to drive a manual car. When you start learning to drive you are very much in a 'conscious incompetent' space. You need to think about whether you have the clutch in and whether the car is in gear, you need to make sure you've let the handbrake out, that you can see out of your mirrors, and that you've checked your blind spot. And you need to make sure you do all these things in the right order.

Over time, you do these things without thinking

– provided you keep using the skills you have developed. If you don't use your skills you can get rusty, and find yourself 'bunny-hopping' down the road, as I discovered when I borrowed my partner's car recently.

Likewise, different networking situations require different skills. Going back to the analogy of the car, my partner's car is European, and so the levers for the indicators and the windscreen wipers are on the opposite sides to my Japanese car. Which meant that the first few times I tried to indicate, I put the windscreen wipers on instead. So being able to adapt to your environment is important. But don't beat yourself up if you miss steps.

In reality, the likelihood is that the only person who will have noticed is you. Everyone else will be focused on themselves, focused on what they want out of the networking, focused on being liked, and focused on making a good impression. When someone is that focused on what they're doing, then they will miss a lot of things.

The trick is to get to a point where you understand that turning up means that you're already successful, and walking into the room means you've won the battle. From there, being able to ask interesting questions will make you very successful in business. When you ask enough questions, you will end up with a bank of them, and this is what you need.

PUTTING IT INTO PRACTICE: TECHNIQUE

Asking The Right Questions

When it comes to personality types, the questions you want to ask high 'D's are all goal driven, business driven, and industry driven. They want to tell you about their achievements. They want to tell you what they're successful at, and why. *When speaking to high 'D's, ask the practical, results-focused questions.*

The high 'I's will appreciate being asked about the most interesting client they have worked with, the most amazing place they have ever done business, the biggest name they have as a client, and the best event they have been to. *When speaking to high 'I's, ask the big, colourful questions.*

The 'C' type people will like it if you ask them about the most complex job they have ever worked on, what made it difficult, and how they overcame the challenges. Ask them about the processes they go through with their clients, and the outcomes. This is what they are interested in talking about. Ask them about the research they have carried out, and they will talk to you for hours. *When speaking to high 'C's, ask the data-driven, detail-oriented questions.*

With the 'S' types, ask if they've been attending those events for long, how many people they regularly see at the events, and who the best person would be to speak to in order to develop relationships and get to know people better. *When speaking to high 'S's, ask the relationship-based, emotion-focused questions.*

It's about having all these questions in your head, recognising which type of person you have in front of you, and working out which of those questions you can use to start a conversation.

You can apply all of these strategies whether you are a high 'D', a high 'I', a high 'S' or a high 'C'. The only thing that will change is your level of comfort when you are talking to someone who sits in the opposite quadrant to you. This means that you have to be much more consciously competent. You can be unconsciously competent with someone with the same personality type as you, because you speak the same language, so it's easy. The danger is that you can find yourself staying with your friends. This doesn't make you money. To network effectively, you need to put on your consciously competent hat, and talk to people who speak a different language to you.

Putting The Relationship Before The Sale

Think about how you are engaging the other person. This means taking yourself out of the equation. It's not something that people naturally do, but it is the reason why I emphasise the importance of making sure you don't go to a networking event with an agenda. Go to make friends. Make yourself memorable, and then the win comes from the follow up. The follow up is something that people rarely do, but it is key to your success.

If you've met someone at a networking event and you've really enjoyed talking to them or found out something really interesting, then follow it up. Following up might include asking someone if they would like to attend a group lunch that you are hosting, or inviting them to go for a coffee.

When you're successful in business then your time is in demand. Hosting a lunch can be a great way to circumnavigate this problem. By getting fifteen to twenty people round a table to have conversations in a relatively informal setting, but still with a focus on business, you can take a number of relationships further at the same time.

When you make sure you connect with people in real-world situations, as well as finding them on LinkedIn and Facebook where you can like and follow their business pages, then you will be getting seen in their digital network and in real life. This means that you can move the conversations forward.

But when you are at the networking event, it's not about you. If you're going to events and making it about you then you are unlikely to have a high success rate. It's the difference between putting the sale before the relationship, rather than the relationship before the sale. The sales will take care of themselves.

Key Takeaways

• Understand your personality type to create more meaningful connections with others.

• To network effectively, you need to talk to people with different personality types.

• Make friends, make yourself memorable, and make sure you follow up.

Chapter Seven

The Generation Game

Multi-generational networking can be challenging. As with networking with different personality types, when you are networking outside your generation it is important that you don't make it about you. If you're going to make friends then you need to meet people where they're at - within reason. To be clear, if someone is being really sexist or racist then you don't want to network with them anyway. In fact I turned down a very large contract with a client once for that reason. It's not worth selling your soul for. Eventually the dinosaurs will die, and that's ok.

However, we're not talking about dealing with dinosaurs here. We're talking about the different ways that different generations deal with things.

I'm in my mid-forties, which makes me part of Generation X. To work through the list that you are likely to encounter in networking situations, we've got the Baby Boomers, Generation X, the Millennials, and Generation Z.

Boom, Shake The Room!

Boomers are at the stage in life and in business where you can expect them to have reached a certain level of comfort. They're fairly unapologetic, and fairly uninterested – most of the time. This means you have to earn the right to be heard.

When you're dealing with Boomers, you need to have stories. They're going to ask you who you've worked with. They want to know your track record and why they need to talk to you. As you're not part of their inner circle the amount of time they will be prepared to give their attention to you will be limited, so you need to be able to succinctly list your credentials and capture their attention.

PUTTING IT INTO PRACTICE: EXAMPLE

OK, Boomer

A close friend of mine, Michael, owns an alarm company. He's lovely. He's also the most politically incorrect man you'll ever meet in your life. But he means no harm.

Michael and I met at a networking lunch, where we were seated next to one another. He quickly adopted me, because I could hold an interesting conversation. This turned into introductions to politicians and a number of other high-powered figures.

Michael is one of those guys who has everyone's phone number. If he rings the Premier of South Australia, then they take his call. He knows everybody. He's been around forever, but he's no dinosaur. He is simply very unapologetic about who he is, and I hope he never dies.

The first thing that Michael did was to tell me that his track record for sitting next to pretty young things and not getting in trouble was not particularly high. I responded that my track record of sitting next to older gentlemen and not speaking my mind was equally low. He told me that he liked people who spoke their mind.

When you pay attention to how someone engages you then you can meet them there. Michael calls a spade a spade, and has a very tongue-in-cheek sense of humour. And zero filter. So if you want to carry on a conversation with him then you have to be the same.

Getting comfortable with being a networking chameleon means understanding when humour is part of the dialogue, and when it's not. Every generation has a slightly different language. This is not only in terms of the words used, it's also in terms of what is and isn't considered to be ok. Understanding how to speak, or at least how to translate these different languages, opens up all kinds of opportunities.

There is another gentleman, Mark Colquhoun, who ran a very large organisation in South Australia. I used to get invited to their Christmas lunches and mall walks every year. They were absolutely beautiful events. After a lovely lunch everyone put $100 in an envelope, and then we all walked the mall. Two people's names had been drawn out of a hat during the lunch, and those two people got to choose who the money in the envelope was given to. The recipient was always just a random person in the mall - to make their Christmas. It was really beautiful.

Mark was a high-powered, well-established businessman. There were thirty of us at the Christmas lunches, and of those thirty people, two were women, myself, and one other woman in her sixties, so she was part of their generation and had clearly earned her stripes. I was thirty-seven the first year I was invited, and my first thought that year was to ask myself how I got there.

I had first met Mark when I heard him speak at a networking event on how you follow up with people after you meet them at networking events. Boomers have a lot of really good advice. They grew up in the era when business was built on relationships. There was no internet. You had to be likeable, and know how to build relationships over time.

Alongside his Christmas events, Mark used to host regular networking lunches. This is where I got the idea for my 'Not A Boardroom' Lunches. Another networking event that he hosted involved having interns from the university come and meet all his business cronies and ask them questions about what made them successful.

One of the things that impressed me most was that he never sent thank you emails. He always handwrote a letter, put a postage stamp on it, and sent it through the mail. While I would like to say I took that idea and ran with it, I didn't. However, it would be a really good way to stand out, particularly with that generation.

PUTTING IT INTO PRACTICE: EXAMPLE

Earn Your Stripes

During his speech on following up with people after an initial meeting, Mark said that if anyone wanted to speak to him, then they should call him, rather than sending him an email. So the next day, I picked up the phone and called him.

I told him that I appreciated what he had to say, that I was a firm believer in never lunching alone, and that I would really like to have a conversation with him about how he'd achieved what he'd achieved in business. So could I buy him lunch? He said absolutely, and that he was free next week on Thursday.

That was how I started earning my stripes, and securing myself a place at the Christmas lunch table. We had a great conversation. I was polite and respectful, because one thing to always keep in mind is that the Boomer generation demands respect. They've earned it.

PUTTING IT INTO PRACTICE: TOOLS

R.E.S.P.E.C.T

Respect to Boomers means that *you don't cut them off in the middle of a sentence.* As a rule, the younger we are, the more we tend to talk over the top of other people.

It is also important to *repeat back to them what they have said*, so that you seek clarification and understanding – this is a good active listening technique across all generations, but is particularly important with Baby Boomers. And finally, *you thank them for their time.*

Time is a Boomer's most valuable asset. It sounds really morbid, but technically they're moving towards the end of their lives, and so as a direct result of this they place more of a premium on how they spend the time they have left. This isn't a conscious thought, but the older you get, how you spend your time becomes more important to you.

After my initial lunch with Mark I was invited

to a lunch that he was hosting, where I met a lot of very high-powered businessmen. I had interesting conversations and asked good questions. I didn't mention my business unless I was asked about it, and then only spoke about it very briefly. As a result, I was invited back to the next lunch, and the next one, and the next.

By sitting at those tables I got to learn about what was important to those people. There were times when someone would say something that was not politically correct. It's part of the language of that generation. Provided it wasn't racist or sexist or horrible, I would mind my Ps and Qs. However, if they said something that went too far, then I would tell them that I appreciated they held that opinion, but that it was not one I shared.

You don't have to sit silent in the face of something you disagree with. In fact, doing so is not helpful to us as individuals. It's important to voice your opinion. If you can voice your opinion in a respectful way and own it (which means that you don't need them to have the same opinion) then you can actually earn a lot of respect.

Generation X

Networking with Generation Xers can be difficult. What's happened with Generation X is that we grew up in a world where the majority of professionals worked nine-to-five jobs. When you walked out of the office you didn't check your emails, because they weren't on your phone. They were on your computer at work. You might not even have had a mobile. If you did, your clients weren't calling you on it after 5 pm. And they didn't call or email before 9 am. So work started and finished at a reasonable time, and then you had downtime and family time.

The challenge now is that work doesn't stop. You can send emails from anywhere, at anytime - and because you can, people do. You can also send messages across different platforms, so your social and business worlds blend together. All of this means that it is hard to switch off.

On top of this, Generation X have been told that they can have anything and everything they want. Gen X are told they can have a balanced family life, be perfect parents, be well-read, have perfect children, be successful in business, be beautifully groomed, and go to the gym several times a week so that we are perfectly toned.

So Gen Xers are stressed. They're in overwhelm. When you meet them at a networking event, it might be the third event they have attended that week. This means you need to connect with them in a way that mitigates some of that stress.

PUTTING IT INTO PRACTICE: TOOLS

Keeping It Real

When you're networking with Generation Xers, it's about being real. *They want to have authentic conversations about things that matter to them.* Depending on the personality type the topic of that conversation will be different, but it always needs to be real.

The easiest way to talk to Generation Xers is to *talk about challenges. Not problems.* Problems take you into dangerous territory, because they open the doors to negativity. On the other hand, by asking what the biggest challenges are that they currently face in their business, and exploring how you can help, you can make a genuine connection.

A lot of Gen Xers are trying to be good corporate citizens and human citizens, so *talking about what they are doing outside work* is always a good way of building the foundations of a relationship.

'Authentic' is the word of this generation. Even so, you can pretty much split the generation right down the middle, between those who are authentic, and those who sell hard in a way that they began doing in the 1980s, and which they've never moved on from. Those people are slick. Their game is smooth, which is the opposite of authentic. They will ask you textbook questions. They've read all the books, all the articles, and all the blogs. Rather than talking to you about what your challenges are, they will look for 'weak spots' that they can then 'fix'.

The Four Circles Of Trust

With Baby Boomers, you're in or you're out. If you can hold your own at a networking event, then you're in. Generation Xers have circles of trust. And it takes a long time to get to the inner circle, where you get to poke around in people's weak spots.

With Gen Xers, if you've just met someone at a networking event then you are going to be on the outside of all of those circles of trust. If you can hold your own then congratulations - you may move to the next circle! However, you'll still have a long way to go. Generation Xers are a lot more distrustful than the Baby Boomers that came before us. The internet hadn't got to them in the same way. For Gen Xers, you need to prove whether you're real or whether you're fake news.

PUTTING IT INTO PRACTICE: TECHNIQUE

A Wheel Within A Wheel

Let's say that there are four circles of trust. The outer circle is about finding out if someone plays at the same level as you. So if you're a brand new start-up, and you approach the CEO of a Fortune 500 and go looking for a weak spot that you can fix, then you're probably going to be in trouble. You'll be left standing on the fringe of the conversation, and you won't be invited in any further.

Another mistake that people make is defaulting to flattery. Don't tell someone how amazing they are. You don't know them! Even if you've read up about them, until you've reached the inner circle you don't have the kind of relationship with them where you get to tell them that they are amazing, and for it to have any real meaning to them. If you go leaping straight to flattery, once again, you'll find yourself stuck on the outside.

However, if you can establish that you do play

at the same level and that you have the same kinds of clients, you may be able to move to the next circle. Once you're in the second circle of trust you can start to have conversations about which industries you work in and what your specialities are. If there are enough touch-points in common, then you can move to the next circle.

The third circle of trust involves repeated contact. Generation Xers need to know that they're seeing the real you, and that you're not just on show. This takes time. You'll need to have contact with someone three or four times, and you're going to have to demonstrate your benefit to that person. Without bragging.

PUTTING IT INTO PRACTICE: EXAMPLE

The Third Circle

One of the ways you can demonstrate your benefit to the person you're looking to connect with is to talk about an aspect of your work that you really enjoy.

If someone asks me what I do, then I will tell them that I have a social media company, and then go on to say that one of my favourite aspects of my job is disaster recovery. I'll explain that when there is a social media firestorm happening it is very emotional and distressing for the business owners, and that I have a proven track record of putting out those fires within twenty-four hours. I'll explain that I really like doing this because I'm taking away the business owner's angst and stress, and I know what it's like to put your heart and soul into your business, so it means a lot to me to be able to help them.

In doing this, I haven't dropped any names by telling them who my clients are. I haven't talked about the last time I solved this problem for someone. I haven't asked them if they know anyone who needs disaster recovery, so I haven't sold anything to them. What I have done is to tell them that I care about my clients.

I would then follow this up by asking lots of questions, and work out a way that I can help them, even if it's just in a small way. I might say that I'm hosting a lunch in a few weeks' time, and that there are people attending who they might be interested in meeting. I'll explain that there's no hard selling at my lunches, but I'll ask them if it would be of interest to them to have the opportunity of meeting those people, and have a conversation with them. Generally, the answer will be yes.

By demonstrating your benefit to the person, without selling to them, you're at a point where you're building a relationship. You can then send them a Facebook friend request. And you're there. You've made it to the inner circle, and at this point you can start asking where their weak spots are, and talking about how you can fix them.

Maintaining Healthy Boundaries

I recently posted on Facebook, saying, 'Some days the world doesn't play the way that I would like it to. Admittedly it doesn't happen often, but today is that day. I think that going to bed is the answer.'

At this point, other business owners started commenting on my post. Those people had earned the right to do that, because we had spent time getting to know one another. They're not my close friends. I have four best friends, and another ten people who I am quite close to. But I have 2,900 Facebook friends.

So making it to the inner circle of someone's business network means you still need to respect the boundaries, and understand that you need to operate within the parameters of a business relationship. But with Generation X, if you've made it to the inner circle, you probably understand this.

If you're very transactional in nature you're not going to get very far. You will probably burn the relationship in the early stages. If you thrust your folio at someone and tell them that you can solve all their problems, or that you've noticed they're connected to a high powered CEO that you want an introduction to, then you're never going to make it to the inner circle. *Relationships take time to build.*

Millennials

The criticism often levelled at Millennials is that they have an overwhelming sense of entitlement. The truth is that everybody does. It's just that we're more comfortable with our sense of entitlement than the way Millennials choose to communicate theirs.

Some Millennials are already business leaders, because the internet has enabled people to start and grow businesses much more rapidly today than they were able to twenty years ago. If you can't speak to Millennials and engage them in a way that builds the relationship, then you're in trouble. Unless you're incredibly rich and about to retire. In which case, congratulations to you, and you probably don't need to read this book. For everybody else, understanding how to communicate and build relationships with Millennials is crucial.

Aside from those Millennials who are already business leaders, Millennials are also your employees, or creating start-ups that are going to go somewhere and achieve things. No matter which bucket they fall into, Millennials have their own networks. So they matter to your business.

Millennials care about things differently and prioritise things differently from the generations that came before them. They do have similarities to those preceding generations, in that there is the same divide between the slick burn and churn operators who just want to get what they want, and those who are looking to form relationships and build networks. So you still need to make those assessments.

Understanding What Millennials Want

Once you have weeded out the slick operators, Millennials are interested in whether or not you're a good human being. They are attracted to success. They want to ask you questions, and they want to be mentored. Which is fair enough. We were all mentored at some stage, and we can easily forget that.

Think about the first manager you had who taught you important aspects of your business, or the university lecturer who imparted wisdom to you. I've developed many members of my team to step up into managerial roles, but when I first started doing it I couldn't understand why it was so hard for them to grasp what seemed like basic concepts to me. Until I realised I had spent twenty years acquiring all those skills.

I worked in five different industries and gained three diplomas, and I was getting cross with people because it was hard for them. That made me a bad teacher. It was nothing to do with the person in front of me.

PUTTING IT INTO PRACTICE: TECHNIQUE

Mentoring Millennials

When you're networking with Millennials it is good to take a mentoring approach - without being condescending. This is the other mistake that people make. As a member of an older generation, it is easy to come across as arrogant when you are speaking to someone from a younger generation.

This happens when people talk about what they've done and what they've achieved, without talking about the backstory of pain that went along with that. If you're talking to Millennials, the level of your current success is not nearly as interesting to them as how you got to where you are.

The relationship between Millennials and Generation X is not dissimilar to the relationship between Generation X and the Baby Boomers. They want to learn. Networking between the generations shouldn't just be restricted to the ones immediately above and below your own, though. It's important for Boomers to understand that they also have a lot to offer Millennials, and that Millennials have a lot to offer them. Millennials understand the internet, for starters.

If you're successful and you've got a great company, but you're in your sixties or seventies and don't really understand how digital marketing works, then Millennials are crucial to your continued success. Those are the kinds of businesses that they run, so it's essential that you know how to get the best out of them.

As with any generation, you need to be selective about who you network with, but the Millennials that fall into this category are really diligent. My Millennial staff all turn up early for work, they all work outside of business hours without being asked – in fact, my biggest problem with my Millennial staff is getting them not to do that. They're also often very detail-driven.

PUTTING IT INTO PRACTICE: TOOLS

Offering Encouragement

Millennials who are business owners, and who have taken that leap of faith, are excited and colourful. They need to be encouraged. *You can provide that encouragement by telling them the stories of your peaks and troughs, and explaining how you got out of the troughs.*

Every business has cyclical pain, and it's never fun when you're at the bottom of that cycle. However, if you're still in business then it means you found a way to get out of it. So tell them the stories of how you overcame your pain points.

Talk to Millennial business owners about things that are relevant to them, such as how finding the right people to hire can be really difficult for a new company. Tell them something that you were told. *Pass the wisdom down the line.* Tell them that no one is ever truly ready, and you just need to leap. Tell them to hire slowly and fire fast. Tell them all the clichés that are so familiar to you, but will probably be new to them.

Above all, talk to them about their dreams. Millennials want to talk about their dreams. They don't want to talk about goals. Often, you will find that their businesses have some kind of a social impact, so ask them about that. Learn the vernacular. Talk about failing fast and start-up grind. Spend some time in the start-up space. But more than anything, talk the language of dreams.

Millennials want to make their dreams come true. They are the fairy-tale generation. They've grown up being able to have it all, and have it all quite quickly. They're the generation where you can push the button and the things are done. They don't understand when they're told it's not that easy.

Sometimes they don't have a filter, but I have found that they really appreciate feedback. Tell them when they're getting it wrong and why. If you can do it politely then they welcome it. If you're focused on building relationships with them then it's important not to dismiss them. However, you can still offer guidance.

PUTTING IT INTO PRACTICE: EXAMPLE

Providing Feedback

I have a millennial friend who is the owner of a social media agency. He's young in comparison to me - late twenties or early thirties. One of his staff emailed me to ask if we wanted their services. I emailed back to say thank you. I explained that I had known the owner of that social media company for a long time, and I was sure if they had a product that could help me personally, or my social media company, or my hotel, that the owner would have reached out and got in touch. I thought that would be an end to it.

I got a follow up email from the employee two days later to say that they could totally set up an appointment for me to meet with them. He just hadn't read my response properly. So I replied, and copied his boss in. I said I appreciated his enthusiasm and suggested he look at the logos in the signature panel of the first email I had sent through, so that he could ask himself if I really fell into the category of their ideal client.

I got an email back from the owner of the company saying he appreciated that I had taken the time and been polite with his very enthusiastic staff. *And this is the point* - you don't need to make people feel bad for making a mistake. But providing feedback is important. There are times, such as with this example, where it's important to let people know what it is you need to say. As a general rule, though, it's important to get permission before providing feedback.

I will often say to people in my network, whether they are Boomers, Gen Xers, or Millennials, that if I could give them some feedback which would allow them to form better relationships, would that be ok? Get permission to give feedback. Until you have permission, they're not going to hear it.

Once the person says yes, you can tell them what it

is you wanted to say. For example, you might say that in your experience, passing a comment on someone's appearance or making a sweeping generalisation (such as saying women are bad drivers) will be costing them money.

These kinds of statements cost business owners money because if you are in a room where fifty percent of the people are women, and you've announced that women can't drive, then they will pick up on this. You might not catch the eye rolls, but they will happen. And it's not just the women in the room. At least some of the men who would have referred female clients to you now won't, because they will have been aware enough to notice the eye rolls.

So the recommendation you make to them is to avoid making comments like this in future. But get their permission before you give the feedback.

Everyone Has Something To Offer

The mistake that older generations often make when networking with Millennials is assuming they don't have anything to offer. But you will learn something from every conversation you ever have. Everyone has something to offer.

I know of some great, young start up business owners who I met four or five years ago, and they're now wheeling and dealing on the global stage, with connections I would give my right arm for.

Because I took the time to build relationships with them, when I invite them to a lunch they are happy to come. And if they have one of their high-flying clients in town then they are happy to bring them along too.

You don't know where relationships are going, so you need to nurture them all.

With Millennials it's about making them feel valued. They want to feel as though their voice is as important as yours. You need to take them seriously. It is useful for your business if you do. Because you don't know where they're going.

Generation Z

This generation is only just beginning to step out into the world, and so they may not seem that relevant in a networking context, but it won't be long before they are establishing themselves in the business world, so knowing how to communicate with them is important.

The challenge we have with Generation Z is that they have grown up on smart phones, so although it is a gross generalisation, there is some truth in saying that their social skills are not particularly honed, in the way that we understand social skills. They have their own set of social skills that they can apply within their generation, but in terms of communicating outside their generation, it can present challenges, on both sides.

Generation Z won't answer their phone to you just because they can see you're calling them. They'll wait for you to send a message or leave a text, and then they'll text you back. But they won't necessarily speak to you on the phone, which can be quite challenging.

In a face-to-face networking environment they are still enthusiastic, in the same way Millennials are. However, the trick with Generation Z is to make them feel comfortable. Ask them good questions and let them feel they're involved. Spotlight them a little bit, but don't keep the spotlight on them in a group environment. Let them be seen and heard, but then move on and let them absorb the conversation.

If you're looking at building that relationship then take the time to flick them a text, an email, or a LinkedIn message. Let them know it was a pleasure to meet them, and tell them that you particularly liked a comment they made. Let them know something they said was relevant. By doing this you will make them feel important. We all like external validation. Particularly from people whose opinions we value.

Generation Z and the Millennials do communicate in a different way to Generation X and the Baby Boomers. They will show you something on their phone that they like that is representative of them, whether it's a video, a post, or a meme. It can feel quite strange to have someone bring their phone into a conversation if you're not used to it. This is because it feels as though they're not engaging, but they are. It's just a different way of engaging.

Gen Z also don't necessarily expect a response to their communication, beyond a 'lol' or a 'thumbs up'. To a Gen Xer or a Boomer this can seem rude. Where's the reply? But to the younger generations, if they know that you've seen their message, and maybe acknowledged it, that's enough. After all, Facebook tells everyone when a message has been read.

If they do reply to your messages then the replies can often be quite brief. Whereas Generation X and Baby Boomers will tend to go into more detail, the younger generations will often only write a few words. They're not really looking for a conversation. They don't really believe in superfluous communication.

On the other hand, they are still learning about how to edit their thoughts. Knowing how to deliver a considered response is a skill that needs to be taught. The internet is not really the place to learn this, and it's not taught in school, so as an employer it is important to pass this knowledge on.

They need to know the impact of opening their mouth and saying exactly what they think. The impact of this is to make the other person feel shut down. This, in turn, will mean that person will no longer want to engage with them. So it doesn't warm the relationship.

The Importance Of Being Honest (And Kind)

As far as Generation Z are concerned, there is nothing wrong with calling it like you see it. However, there are many people who don't have an internalised locus of control, or a belief that events in their life primarily result from their own actions, and so this level of honesty can be upsetting. So an important lesson to pass on to Generation Z is to teach them how to be honest and kind.

Being able to deliver an honest opinion in a way that is kind and can be heard is crucial for any generation. Understanding the importance of how to do this in a business environment, particularly if you are networking outside your generation, is essential. Otherwise, what you have to say will not be heard.

Understanding the ongoing ramifications of what you say and how you say it is so important when you are building relationships. For Generation Z, who inhabit the internet in a way no previous generation has, they are communicating with people all over the world in chat rooms and online gaming situations, and those relationships can turn over extremely fast.

The transient nature of the relationships they have online can translate to the real world, meaning Generation Z can cut people loose very quickly. If you're trying to network with them, or, as an employer, trying to build a team with them, then if you're not teaching them emotional intelligence, you're going to find the relationships don't last.

PUTTING IT INTO PRACTICE: EXAMPLE

Helping With The Basics

Have conversations with Generation Z about things that may seem obvious. Explain about making eye contact. Explain about smiling and saying 'hello' when someone walks into a room, even if you're busy doing something else.

Gen Zers tend not to multitask in the same way the older generations do. They are often quick at performing tasks, and so they may not acknowledge your needs if they are already doing something. In their minds, they know they will get to you once they're done with the job at hand.

But they may not be aware that they need to communicate this to you.

Teaching them that humour is not always advised in a professional situation is also key. *Explaining that there are different layers to relationships is central to ensuring they build towards success.* Because the relationship you start to build today, you may not need today. But it may be crucial to you in five years' time. As with all networking, it's about building relationships that last a lifetime.

With Generation Z, if you can be the person that took the time to help them, didn't talk down to them, and gave them the time to accumulate the emotional intelligence they need to become successful, then once they have their own businesses a few years down the track, the relationship you both need will be there.

Key Takeaways

- Bridge the generation gap by meeting people where they're at – without sacrificing your own values.

- You don't know where relationships are going, so you need to nurture them all.

- Networking outside your generation gives you amazing opportunities to teach and to learn.

Chapter Eight

Stop Yelling At People

What is fascinating to me when I watch a lot of people in business attempt to build relationships and build their networks is that they need their voice to be the loudest in the room. They spend their time telling everyone why their business is so great, and why they are the best fit for their clients.

However, we all know that the best way to make friends is to ask people about themselves. When you are networking it's important to have an understanding of how relationships are formed and developed over time. You can't just cut straight to the chase.

PUTTING IT INTO PRACTICE: EXAMPLE

Getting To Know You

I'm launching a BNI chapter in Gawler, which is a regional hub. It would be really easy for me to tap a couple of my contacts and tell them why BNI is so important, and then say isn't it fantastic there's a new chapter launching in Gawler and they really need to sign up and bring me all their contacts so that I can just get it done.

It's very tempting to do it that way. It wouldn't be very successful, though. Because I would be asking for access to their networks, and I haven't earned those stripes.

Once again, it comes down to playing the long game with your relationships. You're building relationships that are meant to last a lifetime. Those kinds of relationships are built by helping the other person, not by insisting that they help you.

Getting to know people matters. In order to build relationships, you need to have real conversations with people about what their goals, achievements, interests, networks, and skills are. This is something that BNI does really well. There is something called a gains exchange that teaches you how to ask those questions effectively.

It's also not rocket science. What happens when you get people to talk about their dreams? Energetically, they light up, their eyes get brighter, their body language changes, and they get enthusiastic. When you ask them really good questions about their dreams, and they share their thoughts and feelings with you, then you will start building on that relationship.

> ## Top Tip!
>
> If you're an advice giver, like me, then you like to fix everything and solve everyone's problems. This can lead you into treacherous waters. If you ask someone about their dreams, they don't necessarily want you to tell them how they can go about attaining them.
>
> So when you're asking about someone's dreams, it's essential to remember that the person in front of you is the most important person in the conversation. They don't need fixing.

It's a bit like the rescuer model of therapy. Unless you're asked for help, don't offer help. Just have a good conversation. Of course it's fine to share things that you've experienced, but make sure you're not one-upping the other person. This is another way we yell at people all the time. For example, if someone tells you that they've written a book, don't tell them that you've just signed a five-book deal with one of the big four publishing houses for A$2 million.

Space Invaders

Yelling doesn't necessarily involve raising your voice. Although there is that example as well! Not yelling is really just about not being that over-bearing person that creates no room for anyone else to have any oxygen. We've all met that person. It's the person you're trying to escape from at the networking event, party, dinner, or wherever it is that you've been cornered by them. And that is generally how it feels, as though you've been cornered.

This means that having really good spatial awareness in terms of what you're doing to people is very important as well. Particularly today, when we have a much greater prevalence of conditions such as anxiety, depression, and post-traumatic stress disorder. We don't know people's histories when we meet them, so being sensitive about how you approach people allows you to build better networks.

PUTTING IT INTO PRACTICE: TECHNIQUE

Spaced Out

In a meeting or a networking environment, make sure you're aware of the layout of the room, so that you never physically back someone into a corner or up against a wall.

Make sure you have open body language and stances, so that all the people involved in that conversation can exit the conversation at any time, or bring someone else into the conversation at any time. This goes for the space you create physically, and also the space you create with words.

You don't want to be a close talker and physically up in someone's space. Equally, you don't want to be overbearing and talking over the top of people.

Train yourself to perform a little mental health check at various points in a conversation, so that you remember to give someone else a turn. Then wait until you're asked a question before stepping back in. It seems silly, but it works, because it teaches you that instead of thinking about the next thing you are going to say, you can focus on what the other person is saying.

When I'm listening to people, I'm not listening in order to give them an answer, I'm listening so that I can figure out how I can help them. I'm thinking about which networks I have access to, who I know that they could potentially do business with, based on what they're telling me, and how I can make the connection. For example, I will think about whether there is an event coming up where I can put the two people together in the same place.

Once again, it's about being the connector, and always looking for ways to do that, as opposed to telling people they should listen to you because you're really special, and that they definitely want to work with you, because you're really special.

PUTTING IT INTO PRACTICE: EXAMPLE

Peopling

Being the connector takes practice. However, it's in no way exclusive to networking events, so the opportunities to practice are always there.

People seem to think of social settings as not being anything to do with networking, and view networking as simply attending business events. However, the truth is that some of the best networking I do is at barbecues and parties.

My partner Alex and I went on a wine rep lunch the other day. Alex said that I would need to do the 'peopling', as he's not very big on peopling, and he knows that I'm quite happy to people.

I didn't think I would know anyone there, but three of the twenty people who rolled up were people I knew from other lifetimes when I was doing other things. This made it really easy to create a conversation amongst a bus full of what were essentially strangers.

So instead of everyone sitting there quietly staring at their phones or the inside of the bus for an hour and a half while we drove down to McClaren Vale, it meant that everyone started having conversations about business.

We were talking about different reps, and different products that we stocked, and what was challenging in our businesses. It turned out that somebody else had three businesses, so we were having a conversation about that. But at no point did I offer people my card, or say that they needed to use me for social media, or that they needed to come to a BNI meeting.

Once again, you become the glue. One thing that I always look out for is the person who feels most uncomfortable in that scenario, and then I figure out how to help them feel involved and included.

In this instance, there was a young man sitting directly in front of me who hadn't spoken for thirty minutes. He got on the bus, sat down, and stared out of the window while there were all these different conversations going on around him. He was painfully shy.

Once I started asking him questions, it turned out that he managed hospitality for a cinema. I said that this could be really challenging, as you often had to order stuff in that you only needed for one event. I asked him if he found that he had lots of surplus stock. And that was all it took. After that, he was talking freely and joining in with the conversations.

Being the person that brings other people into the conversation is a really powerful place to be. This is because out of all the people on that bus, the shy young man would remember me the most, for the simple reason that I was the one who made him feel involved.

You need to genuinely want to know how you can help. So that when somebody provides an opportunity you can see there is some way of actually doing it, as opposed to telling them that you can solve all their problems and then walking away and not actually doing anything about it.

Promises, Promises

Once again, this is about yelling. When you tell someone that you have all these great connections that would be really beneficial to their business, but you don't take action to help them meet those people, all you're doing is yelling about how important you are.

Helping people is not difficult to do. If it's not appropriate to make that connection there and then, either in person or by sending someone a message on your phone, then I will usually do it just before I leave the event, or when I'm on my way home directly after the event. Once I get home or back to the office, then my world is going to take precedence. At this point, it doesn't matter how good my intentions were towards that person, their needs will not be at the top of my list any more. This is why I'll take action while I'm in the process of getting ready to leave the event.

It's important not to try and make yourself look important by telling people you can make connections that may not come through. Once again, this is yelling. I tell people that I can't make them any promises, but that I'll ask the question for them. You should always give yourself a 'get out of jail free' card. When I ask the question, I usually copy the person in, so they can see that I have walked it like I talk it.

PUTTING IT INTO PRACTICE: EXAMPLE

Walking The Walk

The owner of Colour On Demand, an Adelaide-based print shop, wanted an introduction to the woman who heads up hospitality at the Adelaide Fringe Festival. He asked for her by name. I happen to know her very well. I said that I would send her a message, but I could make him no promises, particularly as the Fringe was in full swing. I contacted her and she said that she would be happy to chat, and asked me to pass her number onto the print shop owner so that he could give her a call.

Where most people fail is that they don't do what they've promised to do. Which is a mistake, because it's amazing how powerful your networks become when you are the person that solves every problem.

Finding The Middle Ground

There is a fine line between not yelling and being a shrinking violet. This is the other mistake that people make. The middle ground takes practice.

If you're naturally a loud human being, it's easy to continue being loud. Equally, if you're naturally quiet and introspective, it's easy to sit back and let everybody else talk. *Neither of those things will get you where you want to go.*

In my book *'Seriously Social'*, one of the points I make is to ask the questions you want answers to. You need to understand that everyone around you has something they can teach you. It's possible that you might not need what they have to teach you for another ten years, but then one day you'll have a meal-ticket in the form of a fact or a piece of information that you filed away from a conversation that you had with someone way back in the past.

PUTTING IT INTO PRACTICE: EXAMPLE

Sowing The Seeds

I was talking to a fertiliser company about their social media. They told me that they didn't bother much with Twitter, as there wasn't much point for them. I said that was interesting and asked if their end consumers were farmers and the agricultural sector. They said yes. I told them that it may surprise them, but two of the biggest groups of users of Twitter in Australia were farmers on tractors and people in the agricultural sector.

The people from the fertiliser company were surprised, so I explained that the farmers and the agricultural sector had their own dedicated chats, AgChat, and AgChatAus, which happened at the same time every week.

I knew this because I was running training several years ago on the Yorke Peninsula, and there were a number of farmers attending the training. They had explained to me that they weren't interested in Facebook or Instagram, but that they used Twitter all the time.

So I was able to let the fertiliser company know that not only had I seen these platforms active on Twitter, but I could confirm from my own experience of talking to people from that sector that Twitter was the place to be.

I hadn't told them what I could do, but by asking questions and listening to what they had to say, I was able to provide something really valuable for their business.

Which means that when they are looking for a social media provider, they will remember that conversation, and it will resonate much more deeply with them than the social media company who just goes in, tells them what they can do, and gives them a quote.

Key Takeaways

• Build relationships over time by talking to people about their goals, achievements, interests, networks, and skills.

• Instead of listening in order to give people an answer, listen to understand how you can help them.

• If you promise to help someone, make sure you fulfil that promise. Your networks become amazingly powerful when you are the person that solves every problem.

Chapter Nine

Feigned Interest Is Not Real Interest

When you're trying to build your networks, you can't fake it till you make it, in relation to having a real conversation with another human being. It can be a one-to-one meeting or it can be a really large networking event, but one of the really obvious things that tells me you're not engaged and that I'm wasting my time is this - your phone is in your hand.

Sometimes I can be guilty of this very crime. If my phone is in my hand then I really don't want to be there or I'm uncomfortable, and the fastest way for me to make myself feel comfortable is to get my phone and stare at my Facebook. If someone is doing this, they have completely disengaged, and they are totally uninterested.

Just because you attend an event, nod, smile, and have conversations with all the people around you, if you've got your phone in your hand, it will be pretty obvious to all those people that you've disconnected.

Another basic one is if you are networking outdoors. I don't often wear sunglasses. The reason for this is that, if I can't make eye-contact with people, I feel as though I'm not able to properly connect with them or that I'm hiding something. So one of the ways that you can really show you're interested in talking to someone is to get out of the glare of the sun and take your sunglasses off.

There are all of the obvious body language ones, such as if you're standing with one foot pointing away, in escape mode. Giving one-word answers is also a good indication that you are not interested in the conversation, that you've had enough, and want to leave. You may well be done with the conversation, but the golden rule is to ensure you stay engaged and give that person your full attention until it is appropriate for you to make an exit.

PUTTING IT INTO PRACTICE: EXAMPLE

You Don't Know What You Don't Know

When I am running social media training events I often ask people to write down all the contacts in my network. I tell them to get a pen and a piece of paper, and write down everybody I know.

Of course their response is always that they can't. The point is that we make assumptions about the people that we meet all the time. We make snap decisions that they offer us no value. The thinking is, *'you're just a pest controller'* or *'you're just a gardener'*.

I know someone who is 'just an electrician'. He wears the same uniform as every other electrician who works for that company. The only difference is that he also owns the company and has a team of twenty people working for him. You could make a big mistake in thinking he was 'just an electrician'. This mistake could mean you didn't have the same conversation with him that you would have with the head of a company.

Another guy I know installs alarm systems. He's worked on the police commissioner's house, amongst many others. So even though he doesn't own the company, he has the contacts.

Unless you've got a crystal ball that tells you who is going to be helpful to your business, *don't assume that someone is not worth your time.* You need to take a genuine interest in everyone you cross paths with.

Feigning interest is not going to work, because you will burn the opportunity. *If you're not interested in finding out about someone, you won't uncover and discover the things that could be really helpful to you.*

Going back to the pest controller, by asking him about the most unusual commercial job he's ever done, if he tells you that he had to control an insect population in a bird sanctuary then this leads on to exploring how this must have been really tricky, as he would have had to ensure he didn't poison the birds.

It's about having your bank of questions, and then really paying attention to the answers. I think what often happens is that if people do have a bank of questions they are usually not particularly useful.

They will ask the other person what they do, if they've had a busy week, or how they're finding the weather. It's really important to have a list of interesting questions that you can ask interesting people, so that they can give you interesting answers.

PUTTING IT INTO PRACTICE: TOOLS

The Human Element

Your bank of questions could include the following:

- Asking someone about the most unusual job they've ever done.

- Asking someone about the most interesting person that they've met through their work.

- Asking what the biggest challenge was in their first year of business.

- Lead into a conversation by saying that you've heard podcasting is growing 70% year on year. Then ask if they listen to podcasts, and if so, who their favourite podcaster is.

  Asking people non-sales related questions, as if you were at a party or a bar is much, much more effective than asking what their turnover was last year or how many staff they have.

Pretend you're writing a biography of that person. Because when you're writing a biography, you're looking for the human element. You're exploring why they do what they do, rather than just asking what they do. *When you take a biographical approach to talking to people, you collect stories that allow you to connect them to other people.* This then opens doors that allow you to share stories. This is a very different relationship.

It also means you can leave that person, head across the room, begin a conversation with someone else, discover that the two people really need to meet, and then you can connect them to each other.

Finding Common Ground

Conversation is a two-way street, so we can turn things around. Say that someone has started a conversation with you, meaning that they are the questioner and you're the person who is being questioned.

You need to be prepared to be open, and a little bit vulnerable. You need to have a real conversation and make a new friend. If the friendship turns into business, then that's lovely. If not, that's also lovely. Some of my best business associates started off as friends first. It's important not to have an agenda. When you don't have an agenda, you don't have to feign anything. You're just there to have a chat.

I found that when I had an agenda, I would often stuff things up. These days, I never have an agenda. It's simpler that way. Going back a few years, my thinking would be that I needed to pick up another four clients. It's hard not to fall into the trap of thinking, 'who does this?' and 'who does that?' But no one wants to get sold to. The minute you start selling to someone, their ears switch off.

The best thing you can do is to find common ground. By asking people what they like to do when they're not working, you will find things that they like that you also like. Which will allow you to have a real conversation. Just because somebody doesn't look like they would have shared interests with you it doesn't mean that they don't. This all goes back to not making assumptions.

PUTTING IT INTO PRACTICE: EXAMPLE

Creating Memories

I'm a little weird in that I only read two types of books - business books and philosophy books. I do read a little bit of poetry, but other than that I'm not interested in fiction.

So if someone asks me what I like to read I'll tell them I enjoy philosophy. This can then open up a whole world. For instance, they might ask who my favourite philosopher is. I can then talk to them about my love of Nietzsche, and recommend 'Thus Spake Zarathustra' if they are looking for a book to help them get their head around the power of will.

By asking just a couple of questions, we can have a conversation about things I am passionate about.

This may then lead onto me talking about the fact that Heidegger's *'Being And Time'* has forever defeated me, but that I'm determined to read it one day, because a good friend, who is much smarter than me, wrote his thesis on it. So when he said that he'd read it, that was it! I had to buy a copy. I've had that copy at home for fifteen years. I've read one chapter. It was hard.

This can then lead onto another conversation, where I have the opportunity to ask about the one thing they wish they could do, but have never quite been able to finish. All of these things access different parts of people's brains and create different conversations. This then creates a memory and an energetic sense around you as a person.

When you've been doing this for a long time it becomes automatic. At first, you need to mentally catalogue the best questions to open with. It's about trying different doors and seeing where they lead. Not feigning interest doesn't mean that you're going to be interested in everything that everyone has to say. It means that you find the touch points where you can make genuine connections.

Conversations will reach their natural conclusion sometimes, so it is also important to know how to exit gracefully. The way to do this is not to say you need to go to the ladies or the gents, even if it seems like an easy way out. It's pretty obvious when you then head to the bar that you were not being honest about what was going on. So you need to be happy to close a conversation.

PUTTING IT INTO PRACTICE: TECHNIQUE

The Great Escape

Start by saying that you've enjoyed chatting, but that there is someone you are very keen to catch up with and so you're going to walk the room for a bit to see if they made it to the event. You can be specific about who you are looking for. I always have a name and an escape plan.

You can say that it would be nice to touch base again in a little while, or that it would be good to catch up for a coffee.

If you're not very comfortable in networking environments it can be easier to stay in a conversation that you're already in even if it's not really going anywhere, than it is to leave that conversation and head off to start a new one.

It's a fairly good indication that you need to exit a conversation when both people are smiling, nodding, and not really saying anything, because neither of you knows what else to talk about.

The kind thing to do in this scenario is to set the other person free. They don't want to be trapped either. They just don't know how to let go! So you need to break up for both your sakes.

Depending on the person and their sense of humour you might be light-hearted about how you end a conversation. You could tell them that you left your wingman on the other side of the room, and need to check in with him to make sure he's still flying. It's always going to be about reading the situation and pitching it to your audience. *And you can't do this if you're looking over their heads*.

Know Your Limits

It can be hard to put all of this into practice. Let's say you've had a really busy day, which happens all the time, and you don't want to go to an event.

If you've already been to six events that week and this is number seven, you need to make a choice. You either need to gird your loins and put your networking hat on, or you need to acknowledge that you don't have it in you. If you truly don't have it in you, then you're better off staying at home.

As much as I always question what the opportunity is that has been lost from not attending an event, if you are genuinely too exhausted or burnt out then it is better not to go than to be there and be disengaged and disinterested. *This is only going to offside people who could potentially be important to your business.*

It's about not ticking boxes. A lot of sales people have networking KPIs, so that they have to attend a certain number of networking events in a certain period of time and then follow these up with a certain number of phone calls to the people they made contact with.

Having networking KPIs is very eighties and old school. Unfortunately, many people who work for big corporates are still caught up in this way of doing things. One of the things that Ivan Misner says that I love is that networking is not a face-to-face cold calling opportunity.

This is the other way that people feign interest. They smile and ask the other person what they do, tell the person that's lovely, announce what they do, hand over their card, and move on to the next person. And so on. Those people irk me, in the same way that speed networking irks me. If you've got sixty seconds to talk to somebody, you're not forming a relationship. You're ticking a box. It may keep the event organiser happy, but I'll be cringing inside the whole time.

The Truth About Networking

Keeping it real all the time is hard. I'm spoilt because BNI is very structured, which is why I love it. Unstructured networking event organisers could often do a better job, simply by having people at the event that they know well enough to trust they will be good at starting and maintaining great conversations. These people could then play at being social butterflies.

Imagine a networking event playing host to eighty people. At that event, there are four social butterflies who are really good at asking open-ended questions and engaging with people who have different personality styles. These social butterflies are the glue. And because they have been tasked with doing what they like to do anyway, everybody at the event has a much better time.

It's a nice idea. However, this is not what event organisers do. Their focus is on selling all the tickets, checking you in, giving you your nametag, and wishing you the best of luck in a roomful of people you don't know.

Networking is not something we get taught in school. So if event organisers are not helping us, then it can be really difficult to learn the skills you need.

PUTTING IT INTO PRACTICE: TECHNIQUE

Stepping Stones

Structured networking events can be a great stepping stone to learn how to do all the things you need to do in an unstructured environment.

Another good approach is to start with small-scale events. By picking events that involve six to eight people catching up for lunch or coffee, or attending forums that are capped at twenty people, you can gradually work your way up to feeling comfortable in rooms of 100 people.

Once you are comfortable in a multitude of different networking environments, you can work out the rooms that are best suited to your needs. I tend to find that the sweet spot is events with about sixty people attending. This ensures there are enough people in the room so that you can have really interesting conversations, and enough people so that you don't get trapped with someone you don't want to get stuck with. All of which means you never have to feign interest.

Key Takeaways

- Even if you're done with a conversation, stay engaged and give that person your full attention until it is appropriate for you to make an exit.

- Find common ground by asking questions and seeing where they lead.

- Know your limits. If you're too exhausted to network well, you're better off staying at home.

Chapter Ten

Community As A Business

Community as a business is a novel concept, in that the way that we do business is continuing to evolve. We are increasingly abandoning the old model that is based on 'numbers, numbers, numbers', 'win at any cost', and 'don't settle'.

A new way of doing business is emerging, which is based on win-win outcomes, and sometimes settling, and being a good human being. Part of being a good human being is looking to solve people's problems, barriers, and challenges.

Social Media AOK has always had the philosophy that the relationship is more important than the sale. You need to consider the relationship first, rather than pushing a solution when you know it's not the best thing for someone's business. Likewise, you don't refer someone in if the person you're referring is not the right fit, just to get runs on the board with somebody else.

The perception of BNI can sometimes be that members refer people in regardless of whether or not they're the right solution. But the successful members, as with any successful business owner, understand that burning your contacts by shoving the wrong providers onto people is not going to help you be successful for very long.

This is because the point is not simply to solve people's problems and challenges, but to *successfully* solve their problems and challenges. In order to successfully solve people's problems, I spend a lot of my time listening to people who are bragging, complaining, and planning.

PUTTING IT INTO PRACTICE: EXAMPLE

Successfully Solving Problems

Two people on a training course I recently ran on email marketing for business were from Seniors Card Australia, which is a discount program for senior citizens.

During a conversation with these people, I said that they clearly had a very large market, and that I'd been reading an article about a new movement happening in the UK, where venues were hosting nightclubs for seniors.

I said I thought it was brilliant, and that I'd very much like to do something similar at my pub, the Duke of Brunswick. I said that I realised that more and more people aged seventy and up were feeling isolated and disconnected, and that they didn't know where to go to make connections.

I said that nightclubs for seniors seemed amazing to me, because the events revolved around music from their era, and that rather than serving a truck-ton of cocktails (although you could still have a cocktail if you wanted one) there were lots of mocktails, high quality teas, and high-end hot chocolates.

I asked if putting on nightclubs for seniors was something we could sit down and have a conversation about. They said that they were really keen to get on board with the idea.

This is what community as a business is all about. Yes, we all want to have successful businesses, but when you're coming from the angle of solving other people's problems, and you're having a conversation with somebody who has your target market, then it's exciting to them. It's innovative and it's different, so they want to come and play. You can be solving problems that they don't even necessarily know they have, and at this point one business can seamlessly dovetail with another, which can then dovetail with another.

So paying attention to what people are talking about and asking about their goals, dreams, and aspirations, enables you to build a community of like-minded people around you. These people will be excited by the things you care about, and they will be happy to think outside the box. This means you can really create crazy, amazing things. *Without paying attention, you don't get to discover that those humans are out there.*

When you are looking to solve people's problems, there are three different stages - bragging, complaining, and planning – that are extremely useful to you.

PUTTING IT INTO PRACTICE: TECHNIQUE

Bragging

People who complain are easy, because you ask them one question, which is this, 'If I put you in touch with someone who can solve that challenge for you, would that be of interest to you?'

If they say no, then that's fine. They are just a person that likes to whinge. However, if they say that would be a lifesaver, then this is where your network comes in handy. You need to have the people in your back pocket who can solve other people's problems.

The trick at this point is to give the person who you are handing that opportunity onto the entire backstory.

The scenario might be that you put in a phone call or drop an email to the person to let them know you were talking to someone at the weekend who is the CEO of a Google Ads company. You can explain that she was complaining that her internet speed is ridiculously slow, so her staff are always losing productivity.

You can let them know that this CEO is a bullet-point kind of person, that she is expecting a call from them on Monday at 10am, so it's important not to be late with the call as she has very limited windows of time in which to speak to people.

So you give them the backstory. The expectation that you have from that person is that they then come back to you and let you know how everything went.

If they were calling the CEO at ten o' clock on Monday, you should expect a call by twelve o' clock on Monday to tell you that they spoke to the CEO, and what the result of the conversation was.

Asking people to let you know how things went with a connection you made for them is about educating your network to understand that you care, beyond just making the connection.

You want to know what the outcome was, if they made you look good, and if the person you connected them to had their problem solved.

When someone gets a referral, their one job is to make the person who referred them look good. If you have just tied your network and your reputation to someone else's, you need to know that everything is good.

PUTTING IT INTO PRACTICE: TECHNIQUE

Complaining And Planning

The complaining people are easy, especially if you have lots of contacts. This means building a network of people you can trust is key.

Planning is always interesting. Somebody may be talking about buying a house, moving to a bigger office, or taking on a new member of staff. So when it comes to planning, you need a shopping list of questions that you can ask.

Exploring what they think the biggest challenge is going to be is a great starting point. What you're doing by asking them this is gently shifting them from planning to complaining. Once you've shifted them to complaining, you can then solve the problem for them.

The scenario might be that they are moving to a bigger office. By asking them what they think the biggest challenge might be, you discover that they are concerned the office fit-out will be a nightmare. This then gives you the opportunity to introduce them to someone who can help them make the fit-out headache-free.

Every time you solve someone's problem, you become the centre of influence for them again. And that's where you want to live. You want oracle status. *You want to be the person that people come to.* When you are that person, it means you are seriously networked.

It might sound terrible to try and get people to the complaining stage, but by doing this you can solve their problems. So asking them what their challenges are, finding out the concerns they have, exploring whether or not they have completed a project like that before, all of these open-ended questions will help you to understand their problems. *At this stage, you're still listening to listen, you're not listening to answer.*

Ultimately, you will ask some clarifying questions, such as finding out where this problem sits on a scale of one to ten. Ask if it's a top priority for them or if it's way down on their list. Find out if it's a short-term goal or a long-term goal. This will tell you how referable somebody is.

PUTTING IT INTO PRACTICE: EXAMPLE

Paying Attention To The Person In Front Of You

I recently met a woman who worked for a data analytics company. They sell embedded analytics solutions, where they take spreadsheets and turn them into visuals that make sense.

Her challenge is that she is both the sales and the marketing manager, and they are in the process of opening up in six different countries. She's trying to take on all this responsibility, because the directors of the company think she should be able to. Which was how I came to meet her. The directors had paid her to come and do some training with me. She was doing email marketing in the morning, and search engine optimisation basics in the afternoon.

At some point during the day she asked if Social Media AOK provide full service solutions. She said she understood that she had come to me for training and coaching, but she was interested to know if we provided full service solutions. I told her that we did. She asked what that looked like, and I explained that it really depended on the client, and was dictated by things like what someone's time-sinks were, and what they were most concerned about.

This meant she was able to acknowledge that realistically, from the training we had done, she could see that she wouldn't have time to carry out certain tasks. She was confident she could come up with the basic copy and content, but realised she wouldn't have the time to do the minutia. She asked if this was something that we could help with, and I said absolutely. We could quote her to rewrite the pages on the website, put in all the meta-tags, and clean everything up.

It was important that I didn't jump in and go through a massive, comprehensive list of our full service, telling her that she needed every single aspect of what we were able to provide.

If her company were paying to send her to training they would not be prepared to pay for a fully comprehensive service, because they would be hoping that she could do it all. So whatever cost Social Media AOK gave her for our services, she would have to sell that over the line to her company.

How you approach these situations is very much dependent on listening and paying attention to the person in front of you. In this particular instance, it was also about paying attention to the fact that the client had let it drop that they were going into Canada, and the UK, and four other countries over the next year.

Given her role in the company, the fact that they were opening in all of these overseas territories meant that she would need to be running webinars, holding Skype calls, and taking on out-of-hours work, so understanding the back story is very important. She certainly needed assistance and support from Social Media AOK, but it was crucial that I understood the level of support she would require, and that she could realistically expect her company to approve.

Where To Next?

Going back to bragging for a moment, we all like to brag. I love to brag. I pretend that I don't. I pretend that I'm a shrinking violet, while at the same time posting about doing 100-kilo deadlifts.

When people are bragging about things, they are revelling in something that they've achieved. Most high achievers are also thinking about where they are going next. So you can very easily tip someone from bragging into planning.

PUTTING IT INTO PRACTICE: TECHNIQUE

Bragging And Planning

If you start by telling someone their achievements are amazing, you can then move the conversation on by asking what their next bucket-list item is. Or what it would look like if they doubled their achievements over the next year. Or you could congratulate them on landing their dream client, and then ask who their dream client is now. Because the person who had been their dream client is now their client, so what's next?

All of this groundwork means you can get to the questions about what experience they have in a particular sector, and how they will identify what their new dream client's challenges are.

From this you can find out if introducing them to someone who works in that sector, who would be happy to have coffee and chat to them about what is unique to that industry, would be helpful to them. Once again, it goes back to helping people. Because in helping people, the sales seem to happen all by themselves, as if by magic. *The focus isn't the money, it's the people, but the money always comes.*

You will meet business people who will tell you that focusing on people rather than money is an incredibly naïve position to take. This is based on the assumption that behind the scenes, beyond the questions that are asked and the help that is provided, the work isn't going on.

So to clarify, the money does always come, but you do have to be an incredibly hard worker. My golden rule is to do what needs to be done when it needs to be done, in order to achieve the things you need to achieve.

PUTTING IT INTO PRACTICE: EXAMPLE

Putting In The Hours

For the book launch for my first book, '*Seriously Social*', I individually messaged 4,000 of my LinkedIn contacts, copying and pasting, and then personalising the message for each contact.

That's how I spent my Monday night. I didn't sell many tickets, but I did get a number of messages back congratulating me on the book, which puts me front-of-mind for all the right reasons.

I had lots of great responses, and with the people who didn't respond at all, in order to be super-diligent I can then go back in and check to see if they can make the launch, and find out if it was of interest or if I was spamming them. You can be tongue-in-cheek with being cheeky.

People can sometimes assume my enthusiasm means I am being flippant, but this is absolutely not the case. It is simply that over the twenty-five years I have been in business, my experience is that if you put community and solving people's problems for the right reasons at the centre of your concern, then everything else takes care of itself. Doors get opened up for you, and people want to help you because you helped them. You have plenty in the favour bank, and you can call it in, because you're not being self-centred.

A Foundation Of Trust

The principles of community as a business are really founded on trust. If you prove to people that you're trustworthy, then they are likely to trust you with their business. With this in mind, there are a couple of cardinal mistakes that people make.

For example, if someone says they are going to do something by a certain date, and they don't, it becomes harder to trust that person. If someone says they will give you an update on figures by a certain time, or that they will call on a particular day, and these things don't happen, it becomes harder to trust.

You have to hold yourself to the same account. If you fail to do something you had agreed to do, it is important to ensure you make up for it as soon as possible.

However, people often don't have those difficult conversations with themselves. So when you burn a relationship you need to be an adult and apologise. Nobody likes to say that they're sorry, but as adults we need to get better at owning our mistakes, apologising for inconveniencing people, and repairing the damage - if possible.

In my experience, if you say that you will do something by a certain date and then don't, you've probably cost yourself the deal with most people. Even if there is a reason why you failed to meet the deadline. You have to be cognisant of who you are building a relationship with, and how they exist in the world. So trust is essential.

In the previous chapters we talked about how to communicate with people in the way they want to be communicated with. Likewise, if you really want to solidify your relationships then you need to interact with people in a business sense in the way they interact with the world.

When it comes to expanding that circle of trust, then behaviour becomes even more important. For example, if you connect two people and one of them arranges to call or meet the other at a specific time, and then doesn't call or fails to show up, it can be a big problem.

This is because they are not only damaging the trust that person has in them, but they are also potentially damaging the trust that person has in you. This can mean that by failing to stick to an arrangement you have made, you could burn two relationships. It's trust, and by extension, respect.

So how do you minimise the chance of having your relationships burned by other people, if you are forever connecting people to one another in order to solve their problems?

PUTTING IT INTO PRACTICE: TECHNIQUE

Managing Relationships

When you are connecting people, it is always important to give those people the backstory. You need to manage both sides of the new relationship, in order to maintain both of those existing relationships for yourself.

So the backstory if you are referring one person to another might look like this...

James is a high 'I'. Very easily distracted, exceptionally difficult to pin down, and quite busy. This means that rather than simply agreeing to have him call you at a particular time, you need to send him a meeting request, so that it's in his diary.

Don't tell him that he can call you any time, because you could be waiting for his call for literally weeks. Or months. Or years. Instead, tell him that you can make yourself available at a particular time.

With high 'I's, it helps to give them a weird time, such as quarter past the hour, or ten to the hour. This sends a signal to them that you are super busy, and they are really lucky to have your time. And then say that you will call them, rather than having them call you.

Letting the people you are connecting to one another know how you manage those relationships will give them the best chance of communicating effectively. This gives them the best chance of helping each other, and also gives you the best chance of maintaining both relationships successfully.

Likewise, if someone were giving you the backstory about me, they would need to say that if I said I would call you at 11 am, then I will call at 10.59 am. So you need to make sure that by 10.55am you are free of distractions. But don't expect Simone to be. And be clear about what you want to achieve from the phone call, because Simone will have her own ideas about what she wants to achieve.

All of this is so important, but as business leaders we often don't give people we are connecting the backstory about each other. This is a huge part of community. In a community, everybody knows everybody else.

PUTTING IT INTO PRACTICE: EXAMPLE

Getting The Backstory

I got a phone call the other day. Someone in my network had set up a meeting with someone else that I knew. They were aware that it was a mutual connection.

Although it wasn't a referral, they'd had a meeting with this person and had been left feeling frustrated, so they called me to say that the meeting had gone really well, that the person had been really interested in everything they had to say, and then at the end of the meeting it had all fallen apart. This person had wanted our mutual connection to commit to attending an event with them, and they wouldn't.

I was able to explain that the person they'd had a meeting with separated from his wife two years previously. He now had a new partner, a two-year-old, and a new baby on the way with his new partner. He was recovering from the cost of his divorce. He was very time-poor, exceptionally committed to his existing networks, and already had a lot of really high-net-worth individuals in those networks.

I said that I may be off the mark, but it sounded to me as though the person who had called me had gone in reasonably hard, with their own agenda, and that now they were going to have to take several steps back.

I went on to say that as I liked them, and they were in the circle of people I was trying to help, that I knew the person they wanted to build a relationship with sponsored a particular football club.

I suggested that the best thing they could do would be to ask if there was any chance they could attend a home game as one of the person's guests. This would give them the opportunity to see the person in a non-business related situation, so that they could be enthusiastic and yell at the football together. I also pointed out that the person would have some of his top-end clients there, as that was what he did. It was his corporate box, and entertaining his clients there was his thing.

I emphasised that if he was able to attend a game then he needed to go in with the aim of making friends, not with the aim of selling. I explained that he was twelve months away from playing the game he was trying to play.

So the backstory was crucial. Without the backstory, he had asked this person to commit loads of time and revenue, and to open doors that he had worked very hard to open for himself, when he had zero runs on the board. With the backstory, he was able to begin making a genuine connection.

People go in without the backstory all the time. They're too busy with the agenda that's right in front of them, and they forget the value of the relationship that's going to last them a lifetime.

It's how we get taught to do business. Go and find the people, tick the box, get them to sign on the dotted line, and move on. It's that 1980s mentality again. It might have worked back then, but we've all woken up. We have different values now. There are some people out there who still use those eighties techniques. I could do it, if I didn't care about whether anybody would talk to me ever again. But if you don't worry about each and every person, you don't know what the opportunity cost is.

The focus needs to be on making friends, building community, and getting to know people, so you have those backstories. Because the backstory is the powerful part.

So if you're at a networking event, notice the pin that the person you are talking to is wearing on their lapel. This might give you the information you need to open a conversation that leads you to understand they have two high-functioning autistic children at home, which can then lead to them opening up about the fact they are a single parent.

It's about being observant and collecting the stories. If you can collect the stories then you can share the stories. This, in turn, enables you to help people. Then the community bends over backwards to help you. Eventually you'll wonder how the magic happens, because it will seem as though you've simply snapped your fingers and all the right people are in your network.

Key Takeaways

- Your aim is not simply to solve people's problems and challenges, but to *successfully* solve their problems and challenges.

- Own your mistakes and apologise for any damage that has been caused to the relationship.

- To prepare new relationships for success, and to preserve your own relationships, give people the backstory when you connect them.

Chapter Eleven

Dream On

There are three aspects to why communicating your dreams makes you a better networker. Before considering the reasons for communicating your dreams, though, think about where your dreams can take you. Where will you be in a year, or five years, when you wake up and all of the things you dreamed about have happened?

It's important to take the time to play the 'what if' game. So, what if you wake up tomorrow and have the perfect job, and your business is perfect? People often get caught up in the transactional nature of what perfect might look like. Let's be honest, perfect is a dangerous word!

However, in my life, the perfect job would look something like this: if I had the perfect job, I would have time to wake up in the morning and walk the dog. My children would have fresh coffee brewing for me when I got back from walking the dog. I would have time to drop my children at school every day, before making my way to a comfortable office where I would be surrounded by happy people. And so on.

So the act of imagining your perfect environment is really about your quality of life, more than anything else, and the harmony of your life, and what that looks like.

For me, quality and harmony involves having the time to weight-train, and then mostly just swanning around having breakfast, lunch, and dinner, and talking to people all day. Funnily enough, I did this exercise eight years ago, and now here I am, in my perfect life, with three businesses, writing my second book.

So you need to know what your dreams are.

PUTTING IT INTO PRACTICE: EXAMPLE

Say What You Mean

I said to my partner Alex, when we were walking to breakfast a few years ago, 'Wouldn't it be fun to have a little pop-up bar with single origin mescals and great single malt whiskies.'

He turned to me, and it was one of those definitive moments, and said, 'Do you ever say anything you don't actually mean?'

And I said, 'No.'

I went on to say that even though I didn't know exactly what this new idea would look like in reality, I knew it would become a reality, because I'd said it. If I say something like this, it means I'm thinking about it in the back of my mind, and once I'm thinking about it I will start to see the opportunities as they arise.

I don't subscribe to *'The Secret'* per se, even though it's very popular. I do believe that the act of imagination cultivates your senses in a way that you start looking for the opportunities to bring what it is that you want into being. Part of this is talking to other people about what your dreams are.

PUTTING IT INTO PRACTICE: EXAMPLE

Daydream Believer

People frequently comment that I must be so busy, because I have three businesses. My reply is to say that I need to do more, as my aim is to have five business by the time I'm fifty, with each of those businesses generating a certain amount of profit each year.

Once I have my five businesses generating a certain level of profit, my plan is to give my financial advisor most of that profit and ask him to do something good with the money. I don't need that much to live on, which means I can be the person who goes and buys libraries for schools.

At this point people are often slightly confused. I explain that my dream is to be that person who walks into a classroom with thirty brand new backpacks stuffed with books for each child. I want to make a difference to people, and because reading is something I'm so passionate about I very much believe that books are an incredible way to make that difference.

So when I'm communicating my dreams, this is part of what I convey. I also explain that I want to be able to take my kids overseas once a year, so that they can experience cultures other than their own, and have a full appreciation of where they're growing up and how lucky they are.

Once you know what your dreams are, you then need to understand what that looks like as a reality.

Getting A Life

Sharing your dreams means you need to have decided what you want to achieve in every area of your life, including physical, spiritual, career, social, family, relationships, and parenting.

There's a really good program called Lifebook, and they have twelve different aspects. They talk about your vision, your strategy, the 'why' of what you're doing, and what you're going to achieve.

I did the Lifebook online program about three years ago. Then I did it again last year, because I got a lot of clarity and self-responsibility for creating those dreams. When you've got the combination of the clarity around your dreams, and you accept that you are responsible for making them realities, you really do start having conversations with people about it.

When you start having conversations with people about your dreams, they want to help. People will buy into your dreams before they buy into you telling them you want an extra A$200,000 a year in sales. They couldn't care less that you want more money.

PUTTING IT INTO PRACTICE: EXAMPLE

The Power Of Dreams

I met a guy called Marcus Teoh at the BNI global convention in Warsaw in 2019. Marcus is a best-selling author on Facebook marketing. I had just given a presentation of the Seriously Social BNI playbook when Hazel Walker, a very good friend of mine, came up to me and said that she wanted me to do a one-to-one with Marcus. A one-to-one within BNI means spending an hour together, learning about each other's businesses and goals.

I gave a big sigh. I'd just given a presentation. We were in Warsaw. All I wanted was to go to the bar and have a drink. But of course I agreed. It was Hazel, and she has done plenty of favours for me, so I was happy to do a favour for her. The irony was, of course, that it turned out Marcus was the one doing me a favour. Not the other way around. Which serves me right for being egotistical.

Hazel arranged for Marcus and me to meet the following morning, which meant that I got to go to the bar. Conventions begin early and it's a full day with a little bit of drinking at the end. So at 8am I was coming down in the lift feeling slightly second-hand, heading to my meeting with Marcus before the day's activities began.

I got to the meeting room and sat down, telling myself that it was ok, and I could get through it. It quickly became apparent that Marcus was being very diligent. He had prepared all his questions, and put a lot of thought into what he wanted to ask me. But he started with his dreams.

He even had pictures of all the different things that represented his dreams. I was so impressed, and humbled. Here was this person who I thought I was doing a favour for, and he was showing me pictures of his wife, and explaining that he'd really like to be able to take her away somewhere nice once every twelve weeks, and be able to give her all his attention without feeling guilty about work. He then showed me a picture of the house that they wanted to buy, and told me that there were a couple of countries that he really wanted to speak in, including Australia.

What it taught me was that you buy into people's dreams. Because in about 1.2 seconds I was saying, 'Oh, I can introduce you to a guy who sets up podcasts in Australia, and maybe he can arrange for you to guest on some podcasts, which might help you pick up speaking gigs in Australia'.

We took a selfie and posted it to Facebook, and it then transpired that he was good friends with people that I was good friends with, because that's how Facebook and the world works.

What it taught me was how powerful dreams are. *Because they connect you to other people.*

PUTTING IT INTO PRACTICE: TECHNIQUE

How To Surprise And Delight People

If you're out networking, look for opportunities to turn the conversation to dreams. You don't necessarily need to start with your dreams - although you'll probably get there during the course of the conversation – but start by finding out what the other person's dreams are.

Make sure you move it away from money, though. Money isn't remotely important, it's just the means of achieving your dreams. So don't spend any time talking about that, find out what they want.

Do they want to sell their business and retire? What do they care about? For example, Ivan Misner is in the middle of studying for his sommelier certification. So when I get in touch with him to thank him for writing the foreword for 'Seriously Social', I will send him a very good wine that will be relevant to his certification. So I will personalise my thank you by weaving it into his dreams.

People's dreams can give you an indication as to how you can surprise and delight them. You don't just want to solve people's problems. You also want to show that you've bought into their dreams.

One great way you can get people talking about their own dreams is by asking questions about their children's dreams. If you find out that someone has kids, you can then ask how old the kids are, and if the kids have shared their ideas about what they want to do when they grow up.

Getting people talking about their kids is pretty much a sure-fire way to make a connection. For the most part, they will only share the proud parent things, which means they will light up.

You can always start the ball rolling by talking about either your childhood dreams, or your own children's dreams.

PUTTING IT INTO PRACTICE: EXAMPLE

When I Grow Up, I Want To Be...

One afternoon my children were on the backseat of the car, discussing what they were going to do when they were grown up. They were talking about the two companies they were going to run, and how many employees they would each have.

Hunter's office would be on the second floor,

and Saxon's would be on the first floor. Saxon then announced that I could be their secretary. My nostrils started flaring, and I turned my head to look at him. He continued, 'You know, when you're not making the world a better place, you can be our secretary.'

My righteous indignation melted away into happiness. I did still let him know that mummy is nobody's secretary, not that there is anything wrong with being a secretary, it's just not what I do.

But the fact that they acknowledged I was making the world a better place, and that they were inspired to have their own companies by the example I am setting for them, meant so much.

Light Up, And Open Right Up

The minute you get people talking about their dreams they will light up, and open right up. At this point, there is no shield. There can't be, because you're accessing the magic, the imagination, and the inner child that wants the big thing.

Once you're in this space with someone there is no filter, and you become much closer to that person much more quickly. Particularly if you let your inner child and your magical person come and play as well. Because then there is fun all round. When you are genuinely excited about all the things that can happen, people will come along for the ride. Which means everybody wins.

Key Takeaways

- Communicating your dreams to other people helps bring what you want into being.

- Dreams connect you to other people. People will buy into your dreams far more than buying into the money you want to make.

- Sharing dreams helps people to lower their defences and let you into their world.

Chapter Twelve

Introverts And Extroverts

We've talked a lot about emotional intelligence, DISC personality types, how to read people, how to ask good questions, and the ways in which different generations like to network. Another way of looking at different types of people in a networking environment is to think about introverts and extroverts.

Most people are familiar with the terms 'introvert' and 'extrovert'. There is a third, less well-known term, which is 'adaptive introvert'. In the context of networking, an adaptive introvert is someone who is naturally introverted and really doesn't like to network, but they can network successfully for short periods of time – preferably in an environment that they're comfortable in – with the right structure. It is for this reason that BNI often works quite well for adaptive introverts.

In Or Out?

When you encounter people, how do you spot whether they are an introvert, an extrovert, or an adaptive introvert? Before anything else, though, how do you identify the type of person you are, so that you can set yourself for success and get the best out of networking? There are some fairly easy ways to health check this.

PUTTING IT INTO PRACTICE: TOOLS

Introverts and Extroverts Health Check

In

If you are an introvert you are more likely to be good in a one-to-one situation, networking in your favourite place. One person at a time is quite easy, because you have control. You can choose when you need to escape, and if you are in a familiar environment you know where the exits are!

Introverts are attracted to structure, which is why BNI is a natural home for them. BNI networking groups have a set time, which means you know when you can escape, there is a finite amount of small talk that needs to be made, and there are rules! Rules mean you can't get it wrong. All of these things are good for introverts.

As an introvert, you may want to arrive at a networking event before anybody else to acclimatise to your surroundings. Equally, you may leave early in order to avoid getting tired and withdrawn.

Introverts' tolerance for small-talk can start to tail off fairly quickly. If this is the case for you then you have to trust that you've had enough. If you've reached a point where it's not working for you any more, and it's exhausting you instead, then you're no longer putting your best foot forward.

One strategy that introverts can use to try and overcome this is to head to the bar. This doesn't help. As an introvert, it's a good idea not to drink at networking events. As an introvert, you are more likely to neck that drink, because you're under stress. You're far better off sticking to mineral water, zero-alcoholic beer, or a light white wine spritzer. This matters, because when you are networking you want to be present. It is better to feel the discomfort and be present than to mask the discomfort and not be fully present.

Out

Being an extrovert doesn't necessarily mean that networking is easier for you. There are extroverts who have high-functioning anxiety. If this is you, then when you are in your own domain you are probably very outgoing and quite content.

However, in a networking environment that feels unfamiliar and where you are not so comfortable, you may struggle. In this situation you may take the role of the joker in the pack, you may be quite loud, or you may make politically incorrect remarks. These are some of the ways you may attempt to assert yourself in an unfamiliar environment.

Extroverts who feel comfortable in most networking environments may want to arrive slightly late and make an entrance. And unlike the introvert who may leave an event early, if you are an extrovert you might feel energised by the atmosphere and stay until the very end in order to continue building relationships over one last drink.

Introverts

Will often arrive early
Find small talk cumbersome
Tend not to hold eye contact
Enjoy abstract discussions
Will gravitate to the edges of a room
Struggle in noisy environments with too much stimulus
Will actively bring people into the conversation
Notices details in conversation that others don't
Easily distracted from the person in front of them
Would rather die than do speed networking

Extroverts

May overshare
Tend to think out loud
Tend to be a social butterfly
Extremely energetic and animated
Tend to speak whats on their mind
Respond strongly to "oddball" stimuli
Enjoy being the centre of attention
Is attracted to people with good stories
Will often spot the new face in the crowd
Will embrace the conversation wherever it is headed

PUTTING IT INTO PRACTICE: TOOLS

Body Language

One thing that can help both introverts and extroverts with being comfortable in their surroundings is to understand open and closed body language. For a start, there is going to be a difference between the people standing by the wall, and those who gravitate to the middle of the room.

Extroverts are drawn to the middle. They want to be where the action is. They want to know everything that's happening. Taking centre stage is going to feel like the place to be. Introverts are the wallflowers. There is a reason why we have the term 'wallflower'. You will find introverts standing near the exits, close to the walls, and in quiet corners - in the parts of the room where they feel under control. Adaptive introverts can flow in and out of all the different parts of the room.

When it comes to how people are standing, if you have two people facing each other, looking directly at each other, they are using closed body language. This means you don't want to go and break up that party. However, if they are standing on an angle, this means that you can come and join the party – they have left room for you to come in.

Understanding how semi-circles work is another good way to ensure you feel confortable.

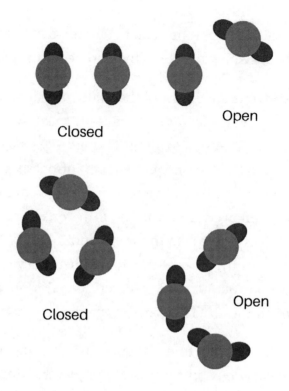

Although in many ways networking is more suited to extroverts, there are still difficulties that can arise for these more outgoing types. As we have already discussed, one of the issues that can arise for extroverts is being very loud.

Being very loud can sometimes mean there is not enough oxygen for everybody else. As a result, extroverts come across as dismissive and abrasive. In a networking situation, if you put an extrovert and an introvert together in a conversation, who is going to give? The master networker will very quickly assess the fact that they have got someone opposite them who is not like them.

PUTTING IT INTO PRACTICE: TECHNIQUES

Energy

Whether you are an introvert or an extrovert, a great way to make a connection is to match your energy levels to the other person. The way you are greeted at the beginning of the conversation is a good way to gauge where to start.

If someone is a bit flat, then you can be more quietly spoken and use fewer hand gestures. You can also go back to your bank of questions and ask them something that is designed to get them talking, so that you begin to raise their energy levels.

To do this, after you have exchanged the initial pleasantries about what you both do for a living, you can ask something along the lines of, 'If I was at a barbecue with your ideal client, what is the one story that I could tell them that would impress them enough to make them want to have coffee with you?'

At this point, they will start to think. And then they'll get animated, because you're accessing the creative part of their brain. As their energy comes up, your energy can come up to meet them. What you are trying to do is leave them in a good place.

Conversely, when you are dealing with someone who is quite loud, the trick is to come in just under their energy level. The reason for this is that extroverts like to have centre stage. Let them. That's fine. You don't need to have centre stage. You're there to make friends. So you come in just under, and when they say something interesting, you become quite animated.

You can do this by doing things like bringing the pitch of your voice up slightly, using hand gestures, nodding, smiling, laughing, and making eye contact. When you do this, they are left feeling important and heard.

In my experience, introverts like to feel as though they have got to know the person they are talking to. Extroverts like to feel the person they are talking to has got to know them. So when you bring these two different personality types together it can definitely be a win-win.

Making Good Conference Calls

If you thrive on being surrounded by people then networking may often feel like a pleasure. For introverts, though, it can be a little trickier. Especially if you're at a conference. So if you are an introvert at a conference, give yourself permission to go and have a nap during the lunch break.

When I was at the BNI conference in Warsaw there were three thousand delegates attending. I just can't do that many people for extended periods of time. The main sessions had two thousand people in a huge exhibition hall. Full of humans. Who are all very excited. So if you're going to a conference, it is a question of giving yourself permission to take care of yourself in that environment.

It's about putting self-care in place, to make sure you're looking after your energy levels and your mental health. Self-care from a mental health perspective is something we don't talk about in business. The reality is that being in business is very stressful. There are two versions of that stress, good stress and bad stress. Even when things are going really well you can still get massive adrenalin rushes that stress your system.

This means that when you're looking at how to navigate through a conference, it's important to give yourself some quiet time and some thinking time. You'll often see people during coffee breaks at conferences sitting in a corner with their laptop open. This means they don't want anyone to come and talk to them. They are preparing themselves mentally to go and do it again after the break.

There are people who thrive on a conference environment. But even for the extroverts, being surrounded by so many people can get tiring. Just because you are an extrovert, it doesn't mean you don't need some time to recharge. Taking on vast quantities of information, which is what you are doing at a conference, is tiring for pretty much everyone.

PUTTING IT INTO PRACTICE: TOOLS

Conference Check List

Giving yourself a check list can be really helpful in a conference situation:

• Do I feel comfortable?

• Have I connected to one or two good people today?

• Have I had good conversations with people and exchanged details?

If the answers to these questions are yes, or if you're feeling overwhelmed, then it's ok to take a break. Go and lie down for a few minutes, or go outside and get some fresh air during a break. Then go back in ready to learn.

Another good trick at conferences is to network differently. At conferences, I network online. As I head into the streams I'll jump on the hashtags and see who has been tweeting or commenting. In this way, I'm in the same physical space, but I'm using cyberspace to have the conversations.

Event organisers who use hashtags are very smart. There are still a lot people who don't make those hashtags visible. By putting them on passes and entry cards conference organisers make delegates' lives much easier. This is because when you are networking at a conference, hashtags and social media handles allow everybody to connect to one another much more easily. Which is important.

It means that during the conference, you can respond to a tweet or a post by saying you agree with the point someone has made, or by saying you thought a certain speaker was amazing. You can then suggest meeting up for coffee and move on. You don't have to have the exchange face-to-face. You don't have to get in the way of the networking they are doing with everyone else. It's about being smart with your time.

You can literally respond to twenty people in the space of ten minutes, and then pick up on these twenty conversations, going into more depth, once the conference is over, and you've got the time and headspace to give people your best.

Key Takeaways

- Match the energy levels of the person you are talking to in order to make a deeper connection

- Create a win-win in conversations with your opposite by understanding that introverts like to feel as though they have got to know the person they are talking to, whereas extroverts like to feel the person they are talking to has got to know them.

- Conference environments can be exhausting. Give yourself permission to take time out to recharge.

Chapter Thirteen

Are You A Social Dope?

People who live and breathe in the networking world can't be cultural idiots. When I was training to be a transpersonal counsellor, one of the things they taught was how not to be a social dope.

In the context of networking, what this means is that you need to understand the cultural context of the people you're likely to be networking with, so that you don't shoot yourself in the foot.

Going back to the example of the BNI global convention, three thousand delegates from seventy-four countries attended the 2019 convention. It was networking on steroids, in terms of needing to get your head around different social norms.

For instance, the contingent from Japan were

highly courteous individuals and very softly spoken. There are expectations, though. So with the Japanese, you need to take their business cards in the right way, and you need to hand them your business cards in the right way. It's also good to know that small gifts which have big meaning are an important way of saying thank you.

With the contingent from Nigeria, which included Abolaji Oyerinde and his lovely wife, I found that the communication style was very tactile. Making physical contact is important, so they may place a hand on the back of your shoulder, or on your elbow, or hold your wrist. So when you are sitting at a table, they may well take your wrist in their hand, make eye contact with you, and talk to you while maintaining that physical contact. It's important to understand that this is just the cultural context of how Nigerians communicate. They're not making a pass.

It's clear to see that reading up on the ways on different cultural expectations and communication styles is going to really help you in ensuring you're not a cultural idiot.

For example, I remember being taught a long time

ago that if you're meeting for a conversation with an Aboriginal Australian that you should sit side-to-side, rather than facing one another. Sitting face-to-face is considered rude.

There are always going to be these little things. Globally, we're all working in cultural melting pots to one degree or another. Just within Social Media AOK I have people from four different cultural backgrounds working with me. Rafi is from Burma, Marie's background is Filipino, Gerel is American, and then there are the Australians.

Now you might think that culturally, Americans and Australians are not so different. After all, we speak the same language. Apparently. However, I have been educated by Gerel and have discovered that actually, Americans conduct business in a very different way to Australians, and they manage their employees very differently. For a start, they don't have awards. It took me a while to get my head around this.

There was an occasion when I told Gerel I wanted to sit down and have a performance review with him and discovered that in America, this was code for getting fired. So there are always going to be different cultural contexts that you need to be aware of in order to ensure you're not upsetting people.

There are some basics that you can easily learn. For example, in some cultures, making eye contact is considered rude. In other cultures, it's expected. However, not being a social dope doesn't stop at societal norms. If you're networking with someone who has Apserger's, they are going to struggle to maintain eye contact with you, but the lack of eye contact does not mean they're being rude.

Not being a social dope extends far beyond not being a cultural dope. Just because someone comes across as abrasive, it doesn't mean they're not a nice person. It can often be that they don't have the emotional intelligence or the filter to know what is and isn't appropriate. They may be very good at what they do, and they often mean no offence, but they have a tendency to say exactly what they think.

In some circles, at some times, having someone who says exactly what they think is very handy. This is because a lot of the time everybody else will be biting their tongue and not being honest with you.

For this reason, I like to have people in my life who have no filters. Because they keep me sensible.

If you don't have any understanding of how to be socially and culturally aware, then do some reading. If you are consistently in networking environments where you are encountering a particular culture, nationality, disability, or minority group, then you need to spend some time to do some research to ensure communication is as effective and productive as possible.

Understanding what is expected of you by different cultures can make a huge difference in terms of whether or not people want to do business with you.

I was speaking to an engineering firm recently, and they were telling me that they had just sent a new shipment of grain processing conveyor belts to Vietnam. They explained that although they could have sent any of their engineers to install the equipment, they understood that the expectation was that they would send their most senior engineer. They knew that this was how to maintain and build the relationship.

Recognising where the relationship started with the person you are going to be doing business with is really important in this context. It really is a combination of social awareness, cultural awareness, and emotional intelligence.

Let's say you meet someone at a networking event. You build the relationship, and they get to know you to the point where they like, know, and trust you, so that they want to work with your company. If you then hand this person off to another staff member in a careless way then you're likely to either lose the work or damage the relationship – regardless of how good the person you are handing things over to is at their job.

It's important to always ask yourself where the relationship started. If it started with you, then you need to understand that there will be certain things you need to do in order to ensure they feel safe, comfortable, and valued if you are going to hand them over to someone else within your business. Essentially, you can't half bake a cake and serve it.

Feeling comfortable with your own cultural norms and expectations is also a part of this. When I first started not managing my diary, I always felt horribly self-important. I would be talking to someone face-to-face and they would ask when we could schedule a meeting, and I'd tell them I'd arrange for Sarah to call them. They would look at me askance.

I'd have to explain that with three businesses, I was at the point where if I put something in my diary myself, I'd break it. I'd learnt that it was better if I didn't touch it, and that everyone benefitted if I left my schedule to someone else.

It felt uncomfortable at first, but after I'd got over my own stuff about not wanting to seem self-important I realised that if you explain things to people then they will understand.

Maintaining your relationships is important, even if they are not business relationships. Because you never know when they might turn into business relationships.

Other than researching specific groups that you regularly come into contact with, it's worth researching the basics. So if you know that there are five main cultures that you are going to encounter in your city, then find out about how not to be a social dope with these people.

In Adelaide, the foreign-born population of the city is about 30%, and includes large British, Italian, Greek, Chinese, Vietnamese, Sri Lankan, Indian, Iranian, and Afghan communities. This means that in Adelaide, it is important to understand how these different people communicate. With some of these groups, you will amass a lot of knowledge over time without doing too much research, but if you're coming off a zero base, then Google is your friend. Get on Google, and read up on the finer points of etiquette in each of these cultures.

The way to do this is to look at articles about travelling to the countries that these people come from. For example, if you wanted to find out about etiquette in predominantly Muslim countries, one of the first things that you would learn is that you don't shake women by the hand. This is a very useful thing to know if you are doing business with a Muslim woman in Australia. If you would like to follow Australian custom and shake hands, then make sure you ask first. Of course many Muslims doing business in Australia understand that this is what Australians do, and so in this context shaking hands with a woman is usually fine. However, you can still score Brownie points by not putting them through the discomfort of something they would rather not do.

The more of this kind of information you have, the more successful you can be over time. It's really about not making people uncomfortable. That is what not being a social dope is all about.

It's also about not being culturally insensitive. Although I am sure there are people who will take the view that cultural and social awareness can quickly become 'political correctness gone mad', I disagree. When you are in business, your job is to be civil, pleasant, helpful, and kind. With kind being the most important of the four.

If this is the case, just because you find a joke hilarious behind closed doors, if it is at someone else's expense, or another culture's expense, or even if it could be deemed to be insensitive, then leave it behind the door. It probably started there for a reason.

Another thing that you often find people doing is making gross generalisations. These are statements that include words such as 'women are', 'men can't', 'the Chinese don't' or 'Muslims always'. When people make these kinds of comments in a networking or business environment, they almost certainly have absolutely no idea what relationships the person in front of them has with the group that they are making a sweeping generalisation about. Whether it's gender, ethnicity, sexual orientation, or whether it's simply that they don't like generalisations or jokes being made about any group of people.

What you can guarantee is this. If you make jokes or generalisations about other people, at some point it's going to cost you money. So the question to ask yourself is would you, rather think you are right, or would you rather have more money? Essentially, do you really need to die on that hill? Or would it be more beneficial for you to swallow your words?

It is often the case that when someone is feeling uncomfortable they will make a joke, because they want to make everyone laugh. The problem is that it is often the wrong joke, and instead of laughing, people are horrified.

A lot of the time this happens because people have never been called out on their behaviour, and so they've never questioned it. The easiest way I can explain this is through a family story about roast lamb.

My gran used to buy a leg of lamb, cut it in half, put half in the pan, and freeze the other half. This meant that my mum would do the same thing. She'd cut the leg of lamb in half, cook one half, and freeze the other half. When I started learning to cook, I asked my mum why we cut the leg of lamb in half. She replied that she didn't know, it was just the way she'd always done it, and that she'd ask gran.

She called gran and asked why we cut the leg of lamb in half. Gran explained that when she had first got married, she'd had a very small oven and a very small roasting pan, so she'd always cut the lamb in half, cook one half, and save the other half for the following week.

Mum pointed out to Gran that she'd had a very large oven and a very large roasting pan for a very long time, so why did she still do it? Gran replied that she'd never really thought about it, and no one had ever called her on it. It had just become this thing that happened in our family, and nearly got passed down through three generations.

Social interactions and business interactions are the same. We learn from the people around us, and the people we grow up in business with. If we don't have good teachers, or we have teachers who are sleepwalking their way through life, which often happens, then we're not going to learn well.

This means that it is very important to question your learned behaviours and biases. It is also important to be aware of when you are feeling uncomfortable in a networking situation, so that you can health check what you say before it comes out of your mouth.

This goes back to the three questions that you need to ask yourself before you say anything, which I covered in my first book, *Seriously Social*.

The three questions are:

• Do I have permission to speak?

• Is what I want to say necessary?

• Is what I want to say kind?

If everyone had to tick these three boxes before they were allowed to speak, there would be a lot less talking.

In any situation where you feel social anxiety or out of your depth, or even just a little bit uncomfortable, these are three really good questions to ask yourself.

I've had some bad role models in my life. In recent history, I've also had some great ones.

Years ago, I had an area manager for a hotel company that I worked for, and I had a staff member who worked for me in one of the hotels, who I had promoted to assistant manager. This staff member's name was Cyril. Now I don't think there's anything particularly entertaining about the name Cyril, but the area manager thought it was hysterical and made a joke about Cyril's name. In front of ten other venue managers I told him that at no time did I find it entertaining that my boss would have fun at the expense of a staff member who worked that hard.

I probably wasn't very popular at the time for making this statement. I also didn't really have permission to speak, but it was necessary and it was kind. In the long run, it also earned me some respect from the area manager. He always minded his Ps and Qs when I was around after that, and I wasn't one of the people he chose to step on when he was stepping on people.

I've also had some amazing role models, who have taught me how to ensure people feel included. This involves recognising how to spot when someone is being excluded, how to recognise when someone is being made to feel 'less than', and how to bring them back into the group.

Inclusivity is a skill you want to cultivate. Whether it is in a personal or a business environment. It's a very powerful tool. Bullies in any environment will only continue to bully if they get away with it. The first time that somebody calls them on it, everybody who witnesses this has permission to call them on it next time.

As we grow up as a society, there are fewer incidents of people being social dopes, but there is still a long way to go. So whether you are educating yourself or the people around you, being part of changing things for the better is going to benefit everyone.

Key Takeaways

• Understand the cultural context of the people you're likely to be networking with.

• Question your learned behaviours, and health check what you say and how you say it.

• Cultivate inclusivity - elevate each and every person to elevate the group.

Chapter Fourteen

No Cup Of Coffee Is A Waste Of Time

The important thing to consider is that it doesn't matter how important, successful, rich, or connected you are - no cup of coffee is ever a waste of time. There are many reasons for this.

Firstly, you don't know who the person you're having coffee with knows. You don't know who's in their network, and who are they connected to.

Secondly, you don't know where your life is going to take you. At any point it may turn out that this cup of coffee is the one cup of coffee that changes your life in five years' time.

Thirdly, you don't know what they know. By catching up for coffee you may learn a little piece of information that you didn't know that will help you to be more successful in achieving your own goals, and taking your business and your life in the direction you want it to go.

PUTTING IT INTO PRACTICE: EXAMPLE

Recipe For Success

Never has this last point been truer than this week. With the Covid 19 restrictions in Australia, the pubs have been closed. I own a pub, which I have talked about a lot in my books. We decided that while the pub was shut we would do some cosmetic renovations. Nothing too extreme, just a little bit of painting and tiling, and that sort of thing.

Part of this was putting a new floor in the kitchen and the cool room. So we stripped out the kitchen. This is a big exercise for a pub, as it means you can't sell any food, and this is currently the only way we're allowed to make any money, through our takeaway service.

The kitchen was only meant to be shut

down for two days, so that we could get back to providing our takeaway service. However, when we ripped up the kitchen floor we discovered that the previous owners had done some fairly shoddy work. They'd bolted stainless steel panels to the walls, but hadn't sealed them properly, so heat had got into the bricks and the floor structure wasn't solid.

When we got to the cool room we discovered that they had bolted stainless steel panels to a very old wooden cool room that was actually rotting and falling to pieces. They'd done a very shoddy job of work, but a very good job of covering up all the issues.

As a general rule of thumb, by the time you find out that all of these things are an issue with a kitchen, you need to speak to the landlord, get them to sign off on everything, then find the tradespeople and schedule in the work. For a normal business, this might be a six-week exercise.

Those normal businesses haven't drunk as much coffee as I have.

The first thing I did was to ring Dion Freda at D Squared Tiling, who is a member of one of my BNI chapters, and someone I've got to know really well over time. As with all these relationships, getting to know Dion started with a cup of coffee. I asked him my favourite question, which is, 'How much do you love me?' This is code for, 'I'm about to ask you a very large favour.' His response was to tell me I knew how much he loved me, and to ask what I needed. I said that I knew he was probably on another job, but could he come to the pub straight away and give me a quote to prepare and tile the entire kitchen floor and walls.

He was on site within two hours. I then asked how busy he was, and how soon they could do it. He replied that they were busy, but that he'd work overnight for me and get it done. So that was the tiling covered.

We also needed a plumber to decommission the gas lines. So I rang Anton, from Brown and Sons Plumbing and Gas, who I've known for three or four years. Anton was another cup of coffee. Anton said that he'd finish the job he was on and be over within the hour, and that he would decommission everything that night, ready for Dion the tiler to begin his prep work the following day.

Part of the process of arranging for all the work to be done was for the landlord to come out to the pub. While he was on site I was having a chat with him, and asked if he knew whether there were any pubs going in Gawler. He said there were a couple, and that he'd go and have a look, and get back to me.

The landlord and I have a really good relationship, and by asking for what you want it can materialise. So it now looks as though we may have a second pub. Most people may think I'm mad, given the current restrictions, but the reality with the virus is that this too will pass.

So it's always about your networks.

The other thing that happened this week was that the South Australian Premier had posted a marketing piece on his social media. I commented that we hadn't been paid our cash grants, which are being made as part of the recovery effort. The response from the Premier wasn't fantastic, so I took a screenshot and sent it to a contact who is in the opposition party. They got back to me asking if I'd like to run for state or federal government.

I don't plan to enter politics today, but this is what your life looks like when you're consistently networking, and having coffee. You make friends with people. And when you make friends with people you are presented with lots and lots of different opportunities.

You don't know where people are going to go. You don't know where they are going to end up in their career. But the relationships you build with them now can be maintained forever.

It's not rocket science. Does it take effort? Yes. Do you have to become good at peopling? Yes. Does peopling take practice? Yes. So practice with the easy people first.

We've talked throughout the book about different personality types, and generations, and introverts versus extroverts, and what all of those things look like in terms of our expectations in networking.

Choose the people that most closely match your personality type first, but at least once a week try and have coffee with someone that you find difficult, and get better at them not being difficult.

Difficult is really just your judgement, and your judgement can get in the way of you building relationships - your judgement about yourself, as well as your judgement about other people.

If I go back ten years, to when I started building my networks, I didn't think I had anything to offer anybody. Nor did I think it was my place to ask to have coffee with the CEO of a company. But if you ask most successful business people, provided you're not trying to sell to them, they're happy to spend time with you and share their experiences. This is because successful business people know how hard it is in business, and so if we can lighten that load for someone else then we absolutely will.

Just remember to put the relationship before the sale, to understand that you're not more important than anyone else, and to respect other people's time. This last point is one of the golden rules when it comes to coffee. Don't be late!

It's fine to be early to a coffee meeting. This shows that you are organised and being respectful of the other person's time, and it also gives you the opportunity to take a breath and get your head together once you arrive. However, being late is never a good move. It either says to the person you are meeting that you think you're more important than them, and that they can wait for you, or it says that you're disorganised and have poor time-management skills.

I'm fascinated by people who are consistently late to meetings but who hold high-level positions of responsibility. You can't get to that level of success and not be good at managing things, so in this instance it demonstrates a lack of respect for the other people attending the meeting.

So because the cup of coffee is the first step to building a relationship, it is good to have a strategy for what to do once you have arrived – early or on time!

PUTTING IT INTO PRACTICE: TOOLS

Questions

I always like to ask questions and to listen to understand, not to answer. I have a range of questions that I like to ask. Essentially, I want to find out why the other person loves what they do, what their biggest challenges have been in the last twelve months, and what the one thing is that they wish someone had told them when they started out in business.

I'll also ask where they are headed in their career, what their perfect life and career look like, and what is the one thing on their bucket list that they'd love to tick off in the next two years.

Back Pocket Questions

1 What are you most scared of right now?

Talking about our fears allows us to see them for what they are. This helps us find ways to solve the issues that led to those fears. By sharing your own fears, you allow people to see you as not just a businessperson, but as a human with challenges, which is what we all are.

2 If your main obstacle didn't exist, what would your life look like?

Find out what is missing from people's business toolkit, and what they need for success.

3 What do you need most right now?

This question is powerful because it helps the person you are talking to prioritise what is most important and needs their immediate attention. It also helps you work out what networks and resources you have at your disposal to help that person.

4 On the other side of this, what will things look like after you have been successful?

This question does two things. Firstly, it helps the person define what they really want out of a situation. Secondly, it tricks their brain into feeling they have already reached their goal. The act of imagining how you feel after having done something brings it into being. It then begins to feel as though the task is achievable.

5 What are the best ways to support yourself right now, and how can I help?

By asking this question you are helping to access the person's subconscious at a deeper level. In counselling we use this as a tool to support our clients to uncover the answers they already have within them.

6 Who will you ask for help along the way? What else will you need?

This question identifies an action-orientated road map to achieving the outcomes the person wants. What resources do they need? What things do they need to put in place? Where are the gaps?

7 What is one key thing you want to achieve at the moment?

This is a short-term win. Uncovering the answer to this question enables you to go through your address books and make some calls or send some emails to help the other person.

8 Tell me about the resources that would be helpful? How or where might you acquire those?

This could be introductions or acquiring new skills. For example, they may be trying to set up an online store or sort out a new calendar system.

9 When you achieve your goal, what will you gain? What will the impact on your friends and family be?

This gives the person insight into the motivating factors behind their goals, which helps to make those goals less transactional and more about the benefits to the relationships they have in their lives.

10 What are the patterns or habits that you need to put in place right now to ensure your success?

Rather than focusing on the negative, this question helps you to programme in and cement the positive aspects of what the person can do to achieve success.

Questions About Goals

1 If your business was ticking all the boxes for you, what would that look like in the next 6 months?

If you understand the answer to this question then you can identify the gaps and help solve some of the person's challenges by making an introduction to someone else in your network. Most importantly, though, it helps you to understand what that person is trying to achieve so you can buy into their dream.

2 What types of clients/ potential referral partners and in what industries do I need to introduce you to in order to help make that happen?

Once you know who it is that can really help the other person, and why it will be a mutually beneficial introduction, it is easier to find a way to open that door and you will be more comfortable in doing so.

3 If you landed your dream client who would they be?

You may know the person they want to connect with, and more importantly we like to help people achieve their dreams.

4 Who in my network can help you take another step towards achieving your dreams for your business?

You are not the answer to every problem, and the most powerful thing you can do in life and in business is connect people to people for mutual benefit.

Questions About Achievements

1 If I connected with your dream client, what's the best story that I could tell them about someone similar that you have helped that will get their attention?

We all like to brag about the people in our networks and how clever they are, but if you are going to be able to brag about someone then they have to give you the story they want you to tell.

2 What is the most difficult problem or challenge you overcame for a client and what was the benefit to the client?

Outcomes count far more than 'what ifs'. By giving you a great example that talks to dollars saved, opportunities won, or a reduction in stress, the person you are talking to gives you something tangible that you can share with other people in your network.

3 If I was bragging about you and your business at a party, what's the one story you think I should tell that people will remember?

Having the answer to this question is a great conversation starter, if the opportunity presents itself.

4 What has been your biggest achievement to date that will help me build your credibility with a potential referral source over other people who do what you do?

If you don't have this information then you are not going to be comfortable suggesting that someone in your network talks to this person over someone else that you or another one of their contacts might suggest.

Questions About Interests

1 When you aren't having fun at work what else do you enjoy doing?

Finding out the answer to this question enables you to discover where the common ground is between you, and also opens doors to networks you may not be aware of.

2 When you socialise what kind of events do you enjoy?

If you understand the answer to this question then, when you are finding ways to put this person together with your wider networks, you will know what kind of setting is going to work best.

3 What does work/life balance look like for you?

This starts a conversation about what's working for that person and what's not, and potentially gives you an opportunity to help.

4 What's the one thing on your personal bucket list that you would love to do in the next 2 years?

Helping someone achieve a bucket list item is an EPIC way to make a great friend for life.

Questions About Networks

1 When it comes to health and fitness what kind of stuff do you do?

This is a great question to ask, because these activities provide networks too

2 What industry associations or bodies are you a member of?

By working out what the person you are talking to is involved in, you can potentially introduce each other to opportunities and people beyond the sphere of your work.

3 (If they mention someone is a great referral source for their business) - **Have you been to any of their industry association mixers or events?**

This may uncover some new networking opportunities that you can look at together.

4 If we were to go to a networking event together to try and find business for each other which event should we go to?

This is a very useful question to ask, because networking with someone who knows your business well and wants to help you achieve your dreams is pretty powerful stuff, and lots more fun than flying solo.

Questions About Skills

1 What specialist skills do you have that are nothing to do with your current career, and which might help me open a door for you with a referral?

People have long and interesting careers, and once you understand their skills catalogue, you can be more creative with your introductions.

2 What unique skills do you have outside of work?

If you know what someone's hidden talents are then it can provide a great way to open a door.

3 Is there something you would love to learn how to do or to master that you haven't yet?

It may be that you are interested in the same things. Alternatively, it might just help you to understand what makes the other person tick.

With all of these questions, you are looking for ways to provide value. If there is a way that you can help the person you are having coffee with to achieve any of their goals then you can solidify the relationship.

When you let somebody talk about themselves for half an hour and you ask them interesting questions, and then ask clarifying questions to the answers they give so that you are sure you have understood them, then manners dictate that they will ask you about yourself.

This means that you get to have a really robust and interesting conversation, *and that is your one goal.* You want to meet someone, face-to-face or online, and have an interesting enough conversation with them so that they want to have another conversation with you, and keep in touch.

Going Forward

Once you've had coffee with someone the next step is to invite them to a lunch. If you can get from coffee to lunch then you've made progress. It should never just be you and the other person having lunch. There is no point in that, because they've already met you. So you invite other people.

Twelve people is a great number for a business lunch. With twelve business owners around a table talking about life and the universe, amazing things happen. People work out that they can do business together. Something always happens at those lunches. The additional benefit is that by hosting these lunches, you are remembered for providing value.

After this, it is about maintaining the personal touch and reaching out to people. One of the challenges that BNI directors are currently facing with the Covid 19 virus is that everything has moved online.

Make It Personal

As an executive director, I have 160 small business owners who are members in my region, spanning a broad cross section of industries. Some businesses are struggling. Some are thriving. Some are working from three o' clock in the morning until eight o' clock at night. I rang every single one of those business owners last week.

Over the course of three days I made 160 phone calls to my BNI members. Some of those people asked if I didn't have anything to do on my own businesses. I have three businesses of my own, and so I always have plenty to do. But the best use of my time last week was to contact, and have a conversation with, every single BNI member in my chapters. Next week, I will contact and have a conversation with every single Social Media AOK customer.

I only ever open these phone calls with one question: 'How are you going?' The answer I get, every single time, is, 'With business?' To which my response is always, 'No, with life, the universe, and all the things. How are you going?'

The minute you ask that question you connect with that person on a human-to-human level. It stops being about business. It is likely that you will be one of two people who will ring them that week without an agenda, just to see how they are. Again, that's a really powerful place to put yourself in a network.

Lose The Hierarchies

One of the things that people are currently asking is what lessons we can take out of the global pandemic. What can we learn, about business and networking? The most powerful people in a network are the ones that remind all the other people in their network that they matter, and that they are the important. The way you demonstrate that is through giving people your time and attention.

Traditionally, most business owners have a top ten of people in their network. As soon as a member of that top ten calls, texts, or emails, they will get a response as soon as practically possible. No matter what the business owner they are contacting is doing. At the top of this top ten there will be a top three, where the business owner will interrupt the person they are talking to in order to take the call.

Powerful networkers – people who know how to weave community around themselves – don't have a top ten. Everybody is of equal importance. Instead of having a top ten you just have rules around what you will and won't do.

People tell me that I'm a workaholic, and that would be a fair assessment. I don't work nine to five. I might take a big chunk out of the middle of the day where I don't work, if it suits me to do that, but I don't let important things wait.

This is the advantage of having digital networks as well as face-to-face networks. I tend to include most of my business connections on one or more of my social media platforms, such as Facebook or LinkedIn. So if someone rings me and I'm not able to call them straight back, then I'll flick them a message to say I haven't forgotten them, and that they are my first phone call the next day. I won't go to bed until I've addressed everything I can, and solved as many people's problems as possible.

The five seconds that it takes me to look up a tiler's phone number at seven o' clock at night, in order to provide an immediate solution for a builder I know, is always worth it. Networking in this way means that when you ask for an immediate solution to your own problem, you are much more likely to receive the help you need.

The Big Coffee Shop

Ultimately, networking is just one big coffee shop where everybody can connect with everybody else to solve each other's problems.

Once you are in that mindset, and you are living your life in that way, so that your life revolves around coffees, breakfasts, lunches, and dinners, then everything is great. Who wouldn't want to live like that?

Years ago, when I first joined BNI, one of the questions that I had to fill in on the biography was along the lines of, 'How will you know when you have succeeded in business?' My response was to say that I would know I had succeeded when I had built my businesses to the point where I was technically redundant, and my only job was to have coffees, breakfasts, lunches, and dinners with people, and to make new friends.

And now here I am, in the wonderful position of being able to share how you can get to this place too.

About the Author

Simone Douglas is the CEO of Social Media AOK, executive director of BNI Adelaide North, publican of the Duke of Brunswick Hotel, internationally renowned keynote speaker, host of the radio show *Seriously Social - The Humanistic Approach To Sales And Marketing* on International Business Growth Radio, and author of the digital networking bestseller *Seriously Social*.

Her strong practical focus on tangible outcomes, combined with an extensive background in business, change management, and process improvement has seen her work with all types of businesses from the local hairdresser through to the Commonwealth Attorney-General's Department. More importantly, her track record of turning random connections and fleeting meetings into robust and proactive relationships that achieve outcomes for her and those in her network is second to none.

Using strategies that draw on her marketing talents, her skills as an executive director of BNI, past training in transpersonal counselling, and her understanding of how to create an award-winning hotel with a strong sense of community and belonging, Simone is perfectly placed to guide readers through the problems and pitfalls that can stand in the way of successful networking.

SIMONE DOUGLAS